# Mothering Through Domestic Violence

*of related interest*

**Making an Impact – Children and Domestic Violence**
**A Reader**
**Second edition**
*Marianne Hester, Chris Pearson and Nicola Harwin*
ISBN 1 85302 844 4

**Domestic Violence**
**Guidelines for Research-Informed Practice**
*Edited by John P. Vincent and Ernest N. Jouriles*
ISBN 1 85302 854 1

**Good Practice in Working with Victims of Violence**
*Edited by Hazel Kemshall and Jacki Pritchard*
ISBN 1 85302 768 5

**Childhood Experiences of Domestic Violence**
*Caroline McGee*
*Foreword by Hilary Saunders*
ISBN 1 85302 827 4

**Domestic Violence and Child Protection**
**Directions for Good Practice**
*Edited by Cathy Humphreys and Nicky Stanley*
ISBN 1 84310 276 5

**Talking About Domestic Abuse**
**A Photo Activity Workbook to Develop Communication**
**Between Mothers and Young People**
*Cathy Humphreys, Ravi K. Thiara, Audrey Mullender and Agnes Skamballis*
ISBN 1 84310 423 7

**Talking To My Mum**
**A Picture Workbook for Workers, Mothers and Children**
**Affected by Domestic Abuse**
*Cathy Humphreys, Ravi K. Thiara, Audrey Mullender and Agnes Skamballis*
ISBN 1 84310 422 9

# Mothering Through Domestic Violence

*Lorraine Radford and Marianne Hester*

Jessica Kingsley Publishers
London and Philadelphia

First published in 2006
by Jessica Kingsley Publishers
116 Pentonville Road
London N1 9JB, UK
and
400 Market Street, Suite 400
Philadelphia, PA 19106, USA

*www.jkp.com*

**Library of Congress Cataloging in Publication Data**
Radford, Lorraine.
Mothering through domestic violence / Lorraine Radford and Marianne Hester.
p. cm.
Includes bibliographical references and index.
ISBN-13: 978-1-84310-473-5 (pbk. : alk. paper)
ISBN-10: 1-84310-473-3 (pbk. : alk. paper) 1. Family violence. 2. Abused wives. 3. Abused wives--Legal status, laws, etc. 4. Mothers--Legal status, laws, etc. 5. Children of abused wives. 6. Child welfare. 7. Abused women--Services for. I. Hester, Marianne, 1955- II. Title.
HV6626.R33 2006
362.82'92--dc22

2006009675


**British Library Cataloguing in Publication Data**
A CIP catalogue record for this book is available from the British Library

ISBN-13: 978 1 84310 473 5
ISBN-10: 184310 473 3


Printed and bound in Great Britain by
Athenaeum Press, Gateshead, Tyne and Wear

# Contents

### List of Tables and Figures

# Acknowledgements

There are many people who have contributed to this book. The research studies on which we draw substantially have been collective enterprises where the work was shared with colleagues and research assistants. These people have, as our co-researchers, contributed enormously to the conclusions and the ideas expressed in this book: (in alphabetical order) Nicola Dominy, Maja Føgh, Lynne Gordon, Julie Humphries, Anne-Mette Kruse, Chris Pearson, Khalida Qaiser, Sarah Sayer, Jo Scott, Nicole Westmarland, Kandy-Sue Woodfield and women from AMICA.

We are grateful for the funding provided over the years to support the various research projects, in particular from: the Joseph Rowntree Foundation, the Nuffield Foundation, Surrey County Council, Roehampton University, Aarhus University, Barnardos, NSPCC and the Home Office.

This book would not have been possible without many people being prepared to give up their time to be interviewed, observed, to complete questionnaires and to otherwise be involved in supporting our research investigations. We have tried very hard to give a fair and balanced account of everything they have told us. We hope that all the people who participated in the research on which this book is based are able to support our conclusions and consider the book and their involvement in the research worthwhile.

# 1

# Introduction

In this book, domestic violence is taken to mean the coercive control of an adult by an intimate partner, involving physical, sexual, psychological and/or financial abuse. Domestic violence is prevalent worldwide, and it has a profound impact upon the health, emotional well-being, life chances and security of adults who are abused and the children who live with them. The language used to refer to this issue varies from the use of gender-neutral terms, such as 'spousal violence' or 'partner abuse', to terms which are gender-specific, such as 'woman battering', or terms like 'family violence' or 'wife abuse', which suggest that violence occurs in the context of a particular relationship (see Radford 2000). Variations in the language used to refer to a problem can reflect broader conceptual and ideological differences. A term can include and exclude, or emphasize, different aspects of the problem. In the UK, 'domestic violence' developed in the context of feminist research and activism since the 1970s, and it is now the most widely used term. It is also the term we prefer to use throughout this book.

We do not, however, wish to mystify the nature of the abuse by referring to domestic violence in a way that also implies gender neutrality. Domestic violence is a gendered crime. Like most violent crimes, it is predominantly men who are the offenders. Although victim surveys and research studies have shown that abuse of a partner can happen in gay and lesbian relationships and sometimes in heterosexual relationships where women use violence against men, women are most frequently the victims of domestic violence – they suffer the most persistent abuse and the most severe injuries (Walby and Allen 2004). Violence is gendered behaviour and it needs to be understood with reference to the power relations that legitimize and sustain it.

The term 'domestic violence' also implies that violence only happens in the home when people are living together, and not after a couple have separated. We will show in this book that this assumption is untrue, and that post-separation violence is a serious problem. Finally, the term 'domestic violence' invokes silo thinking about the nature of gendered violence. It implies that domestic violence is a different species of crime to rape, sexual assault, and the abuse and neglect of children. Available evidence from research shows that this is not the case. Domestic violence, rape, sexual assault, and some aspects of the abuse and neglect of children, especially child sexual abuse, co-exist on a sexual violence continuum (Kelly 1988). The interlinking of these aspects of domestic violence and sexual abuse on adults and children is a major issue that we explore in this book.

*Mothering Through Domestic Violence* is largely based on research we have conducted since the late 1980s into domestic violence, child abuse and children's contact with violent fathers in heterosexual contexts (Dominy and Radford 1996; Hester and Pearson 1998; Hester, Pearson and Radford 1997; Hester and Radford 1992; Hester and Radford 1996a; Hester and Scott 2000; Hester and Westmarland 2005; Radford, Sayer and AMICA 1999). The book brings together some of the major themes we have identified from this research and, although deriving from research conducted in the European context, the themes we explore have resonance with issues and debates that have developed in North America and other industrially developed countries. Our wish to challenge the denigration of mothering, particularly the denigration of abused mothers that can occur in family courts, child protection agencies or as the result of activities by the media and fathers' rights groups, has provided the main impetus for this work. In writing this book, we wanted to reflect on and recount what mothers have told us about their experiences of mothering in the context of domestic violence.

We also wanted to situate recent trends within a broader sociological analysis of gender, violence and power relations. Historically, the needs and rights of children have either been seen to be the same as those of their parents or they have been viewed as at odds with the needs and rights of their mothers (Smart and Sevenhuijsen 1989). This is very much the case today where one area of intense conflict, so-called 'co-parenting' and preserving a child's contact with separated parents, is increasingly being seen as the major equality and children's rights issue to be confronted by the family courts. It is with these complex issues of domestic violence, women's rights and child welfare that the book is centrally concerned.

In the book, we explore how the political battle over children as emotional capital has had a profound impact on the gender entrapment of women living with domestically violent men. The backdrop for the book is the policy context that has developed and shapes our thinking about domestic violence. Domestic violence has had almost unprecedented policy attention in recent years. Since the mid 1970s there has been increasing recognition in the UK and the US of domestic violence as a crime. The criminalization of domestic violence was by the late 1980s beginning to have an impact, especially on police intervention and practice (Hester and Radford 1996b), although the impact on rates of arrest and prosecution has been variable and limited (Hester and Westmarland 2005; HMIC/HMCPSI 2004; Lees 1997). The criminalization of domestic violence has been linked to broader changes in the criminal justice system and tightening of control over crime and disorder – what Garland (2001) has termed a 'culture of control'. Victims of crime hold a central space in the moral justification of the 'tough on crime' approach. This has been an ambiguous trend for feminists and anti-violence campaigners as on the one hand it is a welcome trend for the criminal justice system to be holding domestic violence perpetrators accountable for their abuse. On the other hand, there is a civil libertarian unease about the broader punitive framework, and scepticism about whether or not it all works. Support and advocacy for women experiencing domestic abuse are also essential.

Few believe or have ever argued that the criminal justice system alone can adequately deal with domestic violence. In the UK and the US, we have seen an associated 'criminalization of social policies' so that managing fear of crime is linked in with the policing of poor communities, the regulation of welfare claimants, single mothers, asylum seekers and other people living on the margins (Young 1999). The criminalization of domestic violence has occurred in the context of a liberalist onslaught against welfare services. Women fleeing domestic violence are consequently in more vulnerable positions regards access to longer term financial support and accommodation (Morrow, Hankivsky and Varcoe 2004). Policy trends in one area have undermined reforms elsewhere, often giving a two steps forward and one step backward form of 'progress' (Radford 2000). While the police and other agencies urge women to leave abusers, the family courts lock them into relationships after separation by making unsafe contact orders for children (Hester 2004; Saunders and Barron 2003). In this political context, mothers are set up to fail, individually because of their abusive partner's tactics of control and, more generally, by the policy context that compounds the experiences of abuse. Throughout the book, court case reports, legal affairs and legal publications apply to England and Wales unless otherwise specified.

Questions we address in this book are as follows:

1. How does domestic violence affect mothering? How are the onset of the violence and the dynamics of abuse linked with expectations

about what mothering should be? We investigate how domestic violence affects women's health, resources and overall capacity for parenting. Considering a range of different contexts in which parenting and domestic violence occur, we discuss how living with abuse influences women's identities as mothers.

2.    How does abuse of the mother affect the children and the nature of the relationship between mother, father and child?

3.    How do women cope with and resist the adverse consequences of living with domestic violence, even when a partner deliberately attempts to undermine the mother's relationship with the children? We explore what women are able to do to protect themselves and their children.

4.    Does law and social policy undermine or support mothers who have experienced domestic violence?

5.    What options are there to give mothers better support, to improve the safety and emotional well-being of children and to challenge perpetrators?

## The research on which this book is based

In considering these questions, we will draw upon findings from our research over several years. We bring together findings from six research studies we have completed on domestic violence.

*Domestic violence and child contact arrangements in England and Denmark (the 'contact study')*

The contact study was a qualitative study of what happened with child contact arrangements when women had separated from violent partners. We looked at:

- women's experiences of negotiating and making arrangements for contact
- the practice of professionals and advisors – solicitors, court welfare officers (now CAFCASS [Children's Family Courts Advisory and Support Services] children and family reporters), voluntary sector mediators and refuge workers (and their equivalents in Denmark)
- the effect of contact negotiations and outcomes on the safety and well-being of women and children.

The research developed from an earlier pilot project (Hester and Radford 1992). The interviews were carried out between 1992 and 1995. We looked at the experiences of women in two different national contexts, in England and in Denmark. Although we knew very little about the family law approach in Denmark when we began the research, we had assumed that the strong state support for women as mothers in the Danish welfare system (in terms of good public child care, generous parental leave, better funding for welfare benefits) might also be seen in support given to women separating from violent men.

In the contact study, we wanted to find out whether any history of domestic violence was taken into account when women became involved in negotiating contact arrangements between their children and abusive ex-partners. It made sense, therefore, to take women's accounts of domestic violence as the starting point for our research. All the women in our sample had experienced violence and abuse from their male partners, with about half of them experiencing threats to kill. All had left their partners when we first contacted them.

Questions are often raised about the validity of research based on women's accounts of domestic violence. Courts and professionals working with family law cases nearly always hear conflicting accounts of domestic violence from the parties involved in a case. Perpetrators do not usually see their behaviour as abusive or controlling, at least not in the same way and to the extent that the individual on the receiving end sees it (Dobash and Dobash 1998; Hearn 1998). What women consider harmful differs from what men see as violence or abuse. As Hearn concluded from his interviews with men who were violent to women:

> Men generally define violence in much narrower terms than do women. The paradigm form of violence for men is physical violence. But even here certain kinds of physical violence are often excluded or referred to in passing. (Hearn 1996, pp.27–8)

Drawing on the notion that there are a multiplicity of accounts of the same 'story', it could be argued that women's accounts need to be considered alongside the male perpetrator's, as well as professionals' and children's perceptions of the same events. It was not possible for us to do this in the contact study. Many of the women would have been too frightened of repercussions if we had also talked to their ex-partners. We felt it was important for women to feel safe and not to feel vulnerable as a result of participating in the research. We therefore decided not to interview the violent partners and to concentrate on the experiences of the women, some of their children and a group of relevant professionals.

The contact study involved a series of in-depth interviews and observation work with 53 abused mothers in England and 26 abused mothers in Denmark. All the mothers were faced with making and living with decisions made about the post-separation contact and residence arrangements for their children. We were in regular face-to-face and telephone communication with the mothers for periods of up to two years, seeking ongoing information about the contact arrangements. Some of the women allowed us to observe contact negotiations and/or arrangements. Some allowed us access to their court papers. The observation work and interviews involved substantial contact with the women and the children. We met and mixed with a lot of the women's children but, for ethical reasons, interviewed just two of the children who were living in England. Ideally, we would have liked to have interviewed more children and to have included children and young people from Denmark. Many of the children were very young at the time of the contact cases and were not considered suitable for interview. Many of the older children were under stress or deeply upset by the contact arrangements, and had been interviewed already by series of court-allied professionals; it would not have been appropriate for us to have asked them to participate in further interviews with a research team.

In the contact study, we also interviewed 99 professionals with experience of contact cases in the context of domestic violence. In England, we interviewed 77 refuge workers, solicitors, court welfare staff, mediators and contact centre staff. Twenty-two professionals with similar work experience were interviewed in Denmark. In this book, we focus in detail on the findings from the English contact study, especially in Chapters 2, 3, 6 and 7.

The contact study brought to the fore many examples of unsafe policy and practice and was, we believe justifiably, critical of the approaches taken by the courts and many professionals at the time. We have, however, since maintained a close dialogue with practitioners and policy makers, and carried out follow-up research (Hester 2002; Hester 2005). The contact study has had a direct impact on policy and practice regarding child residence and contact in England, Northern Ireland, Sweden and Denmark. In England, the research was cited as the basis for a number of interventions and amendments during the Parliamentary passage of the Family Law Act 1996, in the adjournment debate on the Children Act 1989 (Hudson 1996) and in the influential family court case *Re L, V, M & H (Contact: Domestic Violence)* [2000] 2 FLR 334.

*Domestic violence in Surrey – towards an effective inter-agency response (the 'inter-agency study')*

This was a community-based, action research study which, taking a needs-led approach, aimed to evaluate and improve on inter-agency responses to domestic violence. The research included a study of the experiences of a random sample of 484 women and 171 service providers, as well as in-depth research into the workings of the 10 locally based multi-agency domestic violence forums. We undertook in-depth follow-up interviews with 23 of the survivors who had specific experiences of different agency responses. Twelve of the 23 women talked extensively about their experiences of mothering through domestic violence, and these data are included in the analysis presented in Chapters 2 and 3.

*Domestic violence: a national survey of court welfare and mediation practice (the 'follow-up survey')*

The family courts in the UK and Europe lagged behind the US in the early 1990s as regards the approach to domestic violence and child contact. Changes began slowly in the mid-1990s in the practice of professionals working with children in the courts; however, as we show in Chapter 7, the trends moved in a number of contradictory directions. Partly as a result of the child contact study, by the mid-1990s, both court welfare officers and voluntary sector mediators started to place a greater emphasis on domestic violence when making assessments and meeting parents (see Cantwell and Nunnerley 1996, p.178; Roberts 1994, p.450). Practice guidelines on domestic violence were developed for court welfare services and voluntary sector mediators.[1] We wanted to take a more extensive look at the practice of court welfare staff and voluntary sector mediators than had been possible in our earlier work, and also to examine any change in practice that had occurred since then.

The follow-up survey, carried out between 1995 and 1997, was based on a postal questionnaire sent out to all court welfare officers and National Family Mediation (NFM) voluntary sector mediators in England and Wales, and to voluntary sector mediators in Northern Ireland. The response rate for court welfare officers was 94 per cent from the court teams (78 of 83 teams responded) and 41.9 per cent from individual practitioners (319 responded out of a total of 761 individuals employed). For mediators the response rate was 94.9 per cent for services (56 of 59 services responded) and 43.8 per cent for individuals (227 out of the total 518 individual mediators responded).

Interviews were conducted with a small sample of 15 mediators and 19 court welfare officers screened through the postal survey, in order to gain more in-depth information on practice issues and to enable further interpretation of the quantitative data. Findings from the survey are examined in detail in Chapter 7.

### From periphery to centre – domestic violence in child protection work (the 'NSPCC study')

Our earlier research on domestic violence and child contact provided a useful framework for understanding the practice difficulties for professionals, especially as regards the identification and monitoring of cases where domestic violence was an issue. Given our own previous work and that of others indicating links between domestic violence and the abuse of children, in this study we wanted to examine how a systematic monitoring of domestic violence by agencies working with children might lead to preventative work with children at risk of physical, sexual or emotional abuse and neglect. We also wanted to examine whether greater recognition of domestic violence in child protection work had any impact on broader inter-agency responses. Inter-agency work can be very challenging and difficult to co-ordinate effectively. Inter-agency rivalry and conflict of interests can frustrate attempts at bringing people together. Agencies have different remits and different approaches that may not marry well (see Hague and Malos 1996). The NSPCC team that participated in this research were keen to develop inter-agency working as they had found, in a small number of cases, that careful assessment of the issues raised by domestic violence created further possibilities for an improved inter-agency response.

The NSPCC research project was carried out between 1997 and 1998. Using a 'reflective practitioner' action research approach (Everitt *et al.* 1992) there was close co-operation between the researchers and the NSPCC team. A monitoring scheme for child protection cases involving domestic violence was developed in conjunction with the team to enable routine enquiry. To map any changes in the practice of the team during the project, a multi-method approach was adopted. This included interviews with individual members of the team, meetings with the team, analysis of 267 case files, analysis of monitoring forms and observation of practice. This multi-method approach allowed some triangulation of data and gave us a method for checking the reliability and validity of results.

This study did not set out to document child contact arrangements but difficulties with contact appeared regularly in the NSPCC's counselling and 'recovery' work with children. Findings from the study are referred to throughout the book.

*Unreasonable fears? Child contact in the context of domestic violence: A survey of mothers' perceptions of harm (the 'AMICA study')*

Chapter 4 outlines the changing debates about child contact in the context of domestic violence during the 1990s. It seemed that attitudes towards mothers fearing domestic violence hardened as women, especially in the UK, were apparently increasingly labelled 'hostile' or 'selfish' and some were even imprisoned for failing to comply with contact orders. Yet at the same time, there was a series of policy and practice changes and influential court decisions in the UK and the US that highlighted the need to take account of domestic violence and work safely with women and children. In 1998, working with the independent women's group AMICA (Aid for Mothers Involved in Contact Applications), a questionnaire survey of 130 abused parents (129 mothers and 1 father) explored parents' fears about and experiences of contact cases involving 215 children. The 130 participants were parents recruited, on a self-selecting basis, through women's refuges, AMICA and contacts with women's centres and women's organizations. For reasons similar to the contact study, none of the abusive partners were surveyed. The research was based on a very detailed postal questionnaire sent to participants. The questionnaire asked about the history of abuse before and after separation, including abuse witnessed by or directly targeted at children, the extent to which the domestic violence and abuse was taken into account when contact arrangements were made, and the impact of contact arrangements on the safety and welfare of the parents and children. Findings from the research[2] are included in the discussion in Chapters 5 and 7.

The AMICA study supported many of the findings from our other research on contact and safety. In this research, we were also able to gain further insight into women's fears about contact and the safety of their children. We consider findings about risk and fears in Chapters 5 and 7.

*Tackling domestic violence: effective interventions and approaches (the 'Home Office meta-evaluation')*

Between 2000 and 2003, the Home Office Crime Reduction Programme funded 27 projects related to domestic violence run by local agencies and multi-agency partnerships. The projects were independently evaluated and a meta-evaluation indicating effective interventions and approaches was produced in 2005 (Hester and Westmarland 2005). In Chapter 9 we draw on the meta-evaluation.

## Who is this book for?

We have written this book for family law, child protection and social welfare practitioners, service providers and policy makers, for services that work with mothers who have experienced domestic violence, for students and for mothers themselves. Aiming for this broad church readership, we hope that we will have been able to address at least some of the key issues for you and offer an opportunity to critically reflect on current policy and practice. This book will not offer you any easy solutions to what are really complex and often seemingly intractable issues. We hope, however, that our efforts may raise some worthwhile debate and make some contribution, no matter how small, to challenging the labelling as inadequate parents of women who mother through domestic violence.

## How this book is organized

As authors, we would of course like you to read each chapter of this book from cover to cover at least once. We have organized the chapters in this book to develop an argument about how different aspects of mothering through domestic violence, taken together, entrap women in gendered violence. Books though have a use beyond the initial reading and we hope that readers may return to sections of the book to re-engage with issues that we raise. This section has been drafted to provide you with a map or guide through our argument by briefly summarizing the themes explored in each of the chapters.

In Chapters 2 and 5, we draw from women's accounts of the abuse from male partners before and after separation. In Chapter 2, we challenge the notion that women who have lived with domestic violence will be inadequate parents. Parenting is physically and emotionally more challenging for women who are abused. It is important for professionals to recognize the impact that domestic violence can have upon women's physical and mental health, and take steps to identify violence and prevent it. However, an overemphasis on women's behaviour as victims has limited thinking about mothering through domestic violence and encourages the view that what women need most is treatment. This puts mothers in vulnerable positions when seeking help from relevant agencies. It precludes consideration of perpetrators' actions, the wider social and political control of women and, most importantly, how women cope with abuse on a daily basis and, in most cases, overcome it. After reading this chapter and our discussion of the policy implications in Chapter 3, readers should be able to apply a perspective critical of mother blaming and talk safely with women about how best to support them in mothering.

We also look, in Chapters 4 and 6, at the (different) understandings and perceptions of domestic violence in legal and professional discourses and professional practices. The material on children and domestic violence discussed in Chapter 4 indicates the circumstances of fear and danger that provide the backdrop for future decisions about children's ongoing contact with fathers after parents separate. Practitioners need to be aware of the complex and often hidden or 'normalized' ways in which domestic violence perpetrators actively continue their power and control over women and children. They need to consider the possibility of maltreatment and abuse to children where mothers are being abused, and vice versa that mothers may be being abused where there is evidence of child maltreatment and abuse. Violence to mothers is an important indicator of risk to children. Without directly asking about domestic violence, it is often unlikely that practitioners will know if domestic violence is an issue for the women.

In Chapter 5, we argue that it is important that practitioners who work with children enhance their individual resiliences and coping strategies. Drawing on research findings, we discuss mediating factors that can boost individual children's coping strategies.

In Chapter 6, we critically review the assumption that children must have contact with fathers, and we show the negative consequences of contact between children and violent men. In this chapter, we argue that it is vitally important that mothers feel safe about visitation and contact arrangements because it is in the child's best interests to have peace at home. In Chapter 7, we further develop the analysis of gender entrapment and litigation abuse by reviewing the law's approach to child contact. Chapter 8 focuses on assessment issues and what factors need to be considered in order to make safe and workable decisions about child contact. A key point we hope to convey in this chapter is the importance of taking account of the traumatic impact of domestic (and sexual) violence upon women and children, and of exploring how living with the domestic violence affected the child and her/his relationship with the parents.

Chapter 9 considers the role of welfare agencies in providing social support to mothers who have experienced domestic violence. Drawing upon research in child protection, we discuss in detail negotiating the delicate line in child protection between supporting and confronting mothers living with domestic violence.

The final chapter summarizes our conclusions and raises questions about further research and the direction of future policy.

## Notes

1   We were invited by National Family Mediation (NFM), the national umbrella organization for voluntary sector mediators, to take part in the development of their national guidelines and training scheme regarding domestic violence.

2   Published in 1999 as *Unreasonable Fears?* (Radford *et al.* 1999).

*2*

# Walking on Eggshells – Mothering Through Domestic Violence

In this chapter, we challenge the notion that women who have lived with domestic violence will be inadequate parents. Parenting is physically and emotionally more challenging for women who are abused. It is important for professionals to recognize the impact that domestic violence can have upon women's physical and mental health, and take steps to identify violence and prevent it. However, an over-emphasis on women's behaviour as victims has limited thinking about mothering through domestic violence and encouraged the view that what women need most is treatment. This puts mothers in vulnerable positions when seeking help from relevant agencies. It precludes consideration of perpetrators' actions, the wider social and political control of women and, most importantly, how women cope with abuse on a daily basis and, in most cases, overcome it. After reading this chapter and our discussion of the policy implications in Chapter 3, readers should be able to apply a perspective critical of mother blaming and talk safely with women about how best to support them in mothering through the adversity of domestic violence.

## Undermining women's health

Estimates of the prevalence and impact of domestic violence vary widely according to the definition of the problem and the methods used to measure it. Government crime surveys currently define domestic violence as including any form of physical, sexual or emotional abuse between people who are or who have been partners in an intimate relationship (Mirlees-Black 1999; Walby and Allen 2004). This definition is broad enough to include men's violence to women and women's violence to men in heterosexual relationships as well as violence to partners in gay and lesbian relationships. The focus of this book is more limited. Our concerns are with mothering in heterosexual relationships when men are violent towards women. In limiting our study this way, we do not want to give readers the impression that violence that occurs in other intimate relationships never happens or is unimportant. It is the gender context of mothering that we are keen to explore, and the research on which we draw has focused on heterosexual mothers.

Crime surveys show that domestic violence is perpetrated mostly by men against women. In the UK, one in four adult women experience domestic violence at some time in their adult lives (Mirlees-Black 1999; Walby and Allen 2004); in the US (Hampton, Jenkins and Vanderfgriff-Avery 1999) and in Canada (Johnson 1998), it affects one in three women. Between one in nine and one in ten women in the UK (ESRC Violence Research Programme 1998) and 1 in 12 (8%) in the US (Campbell 1998) report having experiences of domestic violence in the last 12 months. Domestic violence covers a range of abusive behaviour. It can be criminal and non-criminal behaviour, physical violence, psychological abuse, and sexual abuse and assault. It can be a single act or a pattern of behaviour, ranging in frequency and intensity from verbal abuse, threats and intimidation to manipulative behaviour, physical and sexual assault, to rape and homicide (DH 2005). Research suggests that domestic violence often increases in severity and frequency over time. As we show in Chapter 6, it tends to continue and may escalate after separation. A common factor motivating perpetrators is the use of physically and emotionally abusive behaviour to maintain control and power over the other person (Dobash and Dobash 1980).

The impact of domestic violence varies from person to person, but it can cause great harm to a woman's physical and mental health, affect her behaviour, her economic security and her networks of social support. Researchers are really only just beginning to uncover the costs of domestic violence and its impact on women's health. Research to date shows the following main health effects resulting from domestic violence to women (see summary in Table 2.1):

## Table 2.1: The impact of domestic violence on women's health

| **Premature death** | |
|---|---|
| Homicide | Over 50% of homicides of women are committed by male partners or ex-partners (Home Office 1999; Hampton *et al.* 1999). |
| Suicide | 25% of women's suicides occur in the context of domestic violence (Schornstein 1997). |
| Attempted homicide | Prevalence uncertain. This study found 50% of women who experienced domestic violence said their partners had attempted to kill them, mostly by attempted strangulation. |
| Premature death resulting from ill-health, disability or stress associated with domestic violence | Prevalence uncertain. |
| **Disability** | |
| Permanent physical or mental disablement | Prevalence uncertain. This study found 7% of women permanently physically disabled by the violence. |
| **Physical injury** | |
| Substantial injuries including attempts to kill, stabbing, broken bones, attempts to set person on fire | Survey of 1750 police records in England found 1 in 4 women reported substantial injuries (Stanko *et al.* 1998). One-third of the 65 women interviewed in this study needed hospital treatment for injuries. |
| Knocked unconscious | 10% of women attending doctor's surgery (Stanko *et al.* 1998). |
| Broken nose, jaw, cheekbone | 5% of women attending doctor's surgery (Stanko *et al.* 1998). |
| Broken arms, legs, ribs | 2% of women attending doctor's surgery (Stanko *et al.* 1998). |
| Bruising and cuts | Most frequently occurring injuries (Stanko *et al.* 1998). |

*Continued on next page*

*Table 2.1 cont.*

| Violence in pregnancy | |
|---|---|
| Physical violence during pregnancy | 0.9% to 20% of women suffer domestic violence during pregnancy (British Medical Association 1998). Women battered during pregnancy suffer violence that is more frequent and more severe. They are more likely to be severely injured (Campbell, Oliver and Bullock 1998a). |
| Miscarriages | Women who experience domestic violence during pregnancy are estimated to be four times more likely to miscarry (Stark, Flitcraft and Frazier 1979). Low-birthweight babies, foetal injury or disability of child are also more common (Bullock and McFarlane 1989; Stark *et al.* 1979). |
| Injuries | Injuries include placental separation, foetal fractures, rupture of the uterus, liver or spleen, pre-term labour (Gelles 1988). |
| **Sexual violence** | |
| Rape, forced sex, sexual violence | 40% to 45% of abused women suffer forced sex (Campbell 1998). Injuries include vaginal and anal tearing, bladder and urinary tract infections, pelvic pain, sexual dysfunction, sexually transmitted disease, gynecological problems, psychological harm (Campbell 1998). |
| **Psychological harm** | |
| Depression | 10% to 63% of women experience depression (Campbell 1998). The psychological impact of abuse can take years to overcome (British Medical Association 1998). |
| Post-traumatic stress, panic attacks, fear, nightmares | 63% of abused women in shelters diagnosed as suffering from post-traumatic stress (Golding 1999), 76% report feeling depressed affected their parenting (Abrahams 1994). Stress declines when women are safe (Humphreys 2006). |
| Self-harming behaviour | Higher levels of self-harm, especially among young Asian women who have been abused (Humphreys and Thiara 2003). |

| Eating disorders | (Williamson 2000). |
|---|---|
| Lack of confidence and low self-esteem | (Humphreys and Thiara 2003). |
| **Drug or alcohol problems** | |
| | Women who experience domestic violence are 15 times more likely to have alcohol dependency and 9 times more likely to have a drug problem. Rates of alcohol and drug misuse rise after the first violent episode (Stark and Flitcraft 1996). |

### Premature death resulting from homicide or suicide

Worldwide, domestic violence is a major factor in homicides of women (Daly and Wilson 1988). Women in the UK and the US are at greater risk of being killed by a current or former male partner than by any other person. In the US and the UK, over 50 per cent of female homicides are cases where men have killed their female partners or wives (Hampton *et al.* 1999; Home Office 1999), sometimes after the couples have separated (Wilson and Daly 1998). Domestic violence is also a significant factor in women's suicides. Research in the US found that 25 per cent of women who attempt to take their lives do so because of the psychological trauma caused by domestic abuse (Schornstein 1997). The prevalence of attempted suicide and attempted homicide in a violent relationship is probably higher still, but it is difficult to get accurate data to show this as the reasons for the injury or assault may not be reported nor recorded in agency data (Williamson 2000). We found in the contact and inter-agency studies that half (33) of the 65 women we interviewed said partners had attempted to kill them, most commonly by strangulation (Dominy and Radford 1996; Hester and Radford 1996a).

### Physical injury and disability

The physical harm caused by domestic violence can include broken bones and ribs, skull fractures, internal injuries, knife or gunshot wounds, cuts, lacerations and bruising, burns and scalds, poisoning, asphyxiation and strangulation injuries. Crime survey research shows that domestic violence to women is more likely to result in injuries than are other violent crimes such as theft from the person or fighting in bars (Mirlees-Black *et al.* 1998). Women are more likely to be repeatedly assaulted, to be injured and require medical treatment as a result of domestic violence than are men (Mirlees-Black 1999). Some studies have asked women about the extent of the injuries that resulted. A study of 1750 police records of domestic violence incidents in London England found one in four of the incidents reported substantial physical injuries to the woman (attempts to kill, strangulation, stabbing, broken bones or attempts to set fire to the person). The same study's survey of 129 women attending a doctor's surgery found that ten per cent of the women had been knocked unconscious, five per cent had a broken nose, jaw or cheekbone and two per cent broken arms, legs or ribs. On average, each woman suffered more than four of these substantial injuries although bruising and cuts were the most frequently occurring injuries (Stanko et al. 1998; see also Williamson 2000). Almost a third of the 65 women we interviewed had suffered injuries needing emergency hospital or medical treatment. Just under a third reported suffering untreated physical injuries. A third suffered mostly physical injuries, which they felt did not need emergency medical treatment – they were 'beaten up', bruised or suffered psychological harm.

Research to date has barely considered how many women are permanently disabled by domestic violence. The violence caused severe and lasting physical injury to some of the 65 women we interviewed and seven per cent (5) were permanently disabled. It was clear from the interviews that early identification by medical staff, and intervention before the violence escalated, could have prevented the disablement of these women. Further research is needed to explore in more detail the relationship between domestic violence and women's disability, and the implications for health and mental health policy.

Fear and the partner's controlling behaviour can prevent a woman from getting medical treatment. As a result, many of the injuries resulting from domestic violence are unreported and untreated, or medical help will be sought after some delay. A pattern of multiple injuries, especially where there is a combination of old and new injuries, may suggest abuse has occurred and should always be looked at carefully (Schornstein 1997). The type and location of the injuries can also be an indicator of abuse. Injuries to the face and hands are common (DH 2005). Women assaulted by a partner or ex-partner are 13 times more likely to be injured in the breast, chest and abdomen (McWilliams and McKiernan 1993). An explanation that is inconsistent with the pattern or type of injury should alert a doctor or nurse to the possibility of domestic violence.

## Violence in pregnancy

The reported prevalence of violence in pregnancy ranges from 0.9 per cent within general population surveys to 20 per cent and more for surveys of women living in shelters (British Medical Association 1998). Violence during pregnancy endangers the health and life of the woman and the unborn child. Campbell *et al.* (1998b) compared the experiences of 51 women who were battered during pregnancy with the experiences of 27 women who experienced domestic violence but were not battered during pregnancy. The women who were abused during pregnancy suffered violence that was both more frequent and more severe than the violence experienced by women who were not battered during pregnancy. Women who experience domestic violence are four times more likely to have miscarriages than are women who are not abused (Schornstein 1997). Injuries resulting from violence during pregnancy include placental separation, feotal fractures, rupture of the uterus and pre-term labour. Low-birthweight babies are more common and require more physical care so, on a practical level, they will increase the parenting workload (Bullock and McFarlane 1989; Stark *et al.* 1979). Poor diet and restricted access to ante-natal care also has some impact, as yet not fully explored, upon the health of mothers and children (McWilliams and McKiernan 1993).

## Harm resulting from rape and sexual violence

Violence against women is frequently directed at the genitalia and can be accompanied by sexual acts and assaults which can include rape, buggery and inserting objects into the vagina or anus (British Medical Association 1998). Campbell estimates that 40 per cent to 45 per cent of women who experience domestic violence are forced into sex by their partners (Campbell 1998). Diana Russell's study of rape in marriage found that 14 per cent of the 644 married women interviewed had been sexually assaulted by their husbands and 12 per cent had been forced to have intercourse (Russell 1982). Sexual abuse can cause physical injury to women – an increased risk of pelvic inflammatory disease, sexually transmitted diseases, vaginal and anal tearing, bladder and urinary tract infections, sexual dysfunction, pelvic pain and gynaecological problems (Campbell 1998) – as well as considerable psychological harm.

## Psychological effects

The psychological harm resulting from domestic violence includes distress, fear, depression, anxiety, post-traumatic stress disorder and suicide. The prevalence of depression among abused women ranges from 10 per cent to 31 per cent in surveys of the general population, with up to 63 per cent of women showing signs of depression in research studies of women living in shelters (Campbell 1998). Persons suffering from post-traumatic stress disorder may feel anxious, helpless, afraid, ashamed, demoralized and angry. They may experience difficulties in concentrating, suffer from nightmares, sleeplessness, panic attacks and flashbacks reliving the event. They may have a physical reaction, such as nausea, which is triggered by an event or experience that has become associated with the abuse. They may experience stress-related symptoms such as headaches (British Medical Association 1998). Women who have experienced domestic violence may suffer from a lack of self-esteem and feelings of loss and inadequacy (Hampton *et al.* 1999). The psychological impact of abuse is often said to have the most devastating effect on the victim's health and well-being and can take years to overcome (British Medical Association 1998).

### Drug or alcohol dependencies

In a study of hospital records, Stark and Flitcraft (1996) found that women who had experienced domestic violence were 15 times more likely to abuse alcohol and nine times more likely to abuse drugs. Rates of drug and alcohol abuse rose after the first episode of violence and may have been a consequence of the abuse – an attempt to cope with the abuse – rather than a pre-existing problem in the relationship.

This brief resume of the research findings shows that domestic violence can have a dire impact upon the health of women. Steps need to be taken in relevant agencies to ensure women feel safe to disclose experiences of domestic violence at an early stage in the relationship, and that they are supported in a non-threatening way. This resume also shows that not all women who live with domestic violence will experience poor health, nor will the violence inevitably escalate towards lethality. Many women resist or 'manage' the violence they experience in their everyday lives. Even in situations where violence harms the woman's health, this may not mean that she becomes an inadequate parent. The research on health and domestic violence has been useful for medics and practitioners identifying signs of abuse. But the literature has focused more on objectively measurable physical injuries than on the emotional harm caused by abuse. Looking on the harm alone, while important, raises problems because it tends to focus attention on the victim and her attributes and can divert attention from the broader processes of victimization, especially the behaviour of the perpetrator and the social construction of his responsibility in the broader socio-legal context. Less attention has been given to exploring the ways in which violence is used by abusers to undermine a woman's sense of self-worth and identity as a parent, her confidence in mothering and her relationship with her children.

## Domestic violence, poor health and parenting stress

In our own research with mothers, some of the women interviewed found caring for children more stressful because of the violence:

> You're under a lot of stress. It's like I've got less patient now. I used to be really placid…but I've got less patience and I blow up at the kids more. ('Madeleine')

> He's a very difficult child…it does my head in and I don't know why I can't cope with it but I think I am still stressed. ('Marsha')

But it was not the physical severity and frequency of the domestic violence that mostly created problems for women's parenting. The majority, 32 women, mentioned no effects from the violence on their parenting or on their relationships with children. This finding that the majority of women actually cope quite well and successfully parent through domestic violence is supported by research in the US by Chris Sullivan and her colleagues (1999). Studies comparing battered and non-battered women (Holden *et al.* 1998) have found no major differences in parenting, apart from in the area of maternal stress and aggression towards children. In Holden *et al.*'s study, 92 per cent of the 30 women who had experienced abuse reported using aggressive behaviour towards their children compared with 50 per cent of the 28 women who had not been abused. Aggressive behaviour by women however declined significantly six months after leaving the shelter, with 34 per cent then reporting some aggression towards their children. A survey of mothers attending family centres in England similarly found that a number of them had lost confidence in their mothering, were emotionally drained and distant, felt they had little to give their children and at times took out their frustrations on them. These feelings were compounded by the difficult behaviour of the children at a time when they too could be trying to come to terms with the violence they were witnessing or experiencing (Abrahams 1994). Coping with the behaviour of children who have lived with domestic violence can be difficult for women without social support (Sullivan *et al.* 1999). Our interviews further confirm the importance of social support. Women who were more isolated by their partners, or as a result of poverty and recent migration, reported more parenting stress.

Twenty-three of the women we interviewed said that the violence had adversely affected their mothering. About the same proportions had experienced potentially lethal violence (11 had experienced threats and attempts to kill) as those who reported violence that was not immediately life threatening (12). Even when faced with life-threatening violence, some women said they were able to cope adequately with mothering, and described their partners as 'good fathers' who were 'adored' by their children. It is possible that both parents believe they successfully shield children from even the most extreme forms of violence. It is also possible that women underestimate the impact of the violence upon themselves and upon the children as a way of coping with the abuse, gaining strength in the face of adversity. However, even potentially lethal and frequent physical violence did not always go hand-in-hand with the partner's intense efforts to undermine the mother-child relationship. As we show in the next section of this chapter, the father's deliberate undermining of the mother's relationship with the children had the greatest impact upon women's confidence in their mothering, especially where women had no help and support outside the relationship to boost parenting. A key theme of this book is that in order to support women mothering through domestic violence, we also have to challenge violent men. We need to understand the dynamics of power and control in abusive relationships and the often deliberate targeting of women's experiences of mothering by violent men. In the next section of this chapter, we consider these issues.

## Power and control and the abuse of women as mothers

Beth Richie's notion of gender entrapment (Richie 1995) provides a useful framework for exploring domestic violence and mothering. Richie uses the term gender entrapment to explain why some black African-American battered women living in poverty in the US may turn to crime. Richie's text is important for identifying the interlinking of violence against women with racism, social exclusion and crime. Gender entrapment refers to a process where African-American women are 'set up to fail' in their relationships and in their life ambitions as a consequence of being marginalized by the inter-sectional disadvantages of living through violence, racism, sexism and poverty. In detailed interviews with women in jail, Richie looked at how a woman's sense of identity, her personal life experience (especially in the family and in relationships), her community and culture and the broader institutional structures in which she lives – poverty, social exclusion, racism and sexism – all intersect to influence the process of gender entrapment. Because of gender entrapment, black African-American battered women are more likely to turn to crime as a survival strategy, and they are more likely to be caught. Culture and community can play a key role in a black woman's feelings about making her relationship work, staying with a partner because she does not want a relationship to 'fail' or children to grow up without a father. On the other hand, a shortage of options and services to help black women find safety and accommodation can make it harder to leave should she decide to do so. Poverty compounded by domestic violence can leave an abused black African-American woman more exposed to crimes such as drug dealing or fraud. Gender entrapment highlights how women's experiences of violence differ according to their specific circumstances and the complex interplay between racism, sexism and poverty. We are using the idea of gender entrapment in this book to look at the marginalization and 'failure' of battered women as mothers. Gender entrapment is a useful idea because it allows us to look at not just the affects of violence (harm to health) and what violent men do to entrap women and how women respond, but also the broader social, cultural and political context influencing how women see themselves as mothers and their partners as fathers.

To understand gender entrapment, we need to look at how violent men attempt to gain power and control over women through their mothering of children. Figure 2.1 illustrates the various strategies violent men use to undermine women as mothers and to divert attention from their own responsibilities as fathers and as partners in a relationship. This builds on the earlier discussion of domestic violence and the harm caused to women's health and well-being to illustrate how men direct efforts to control women and children in the family and post-separation towards women's experiences of mothering and their identities as 'good enough' or as 'failed' mothers. Men's behaviour in abusing women as mothers is reinforced and magnified by practices of professionals in the courts and child protection agencies.

## Becoming a mother

Women with children are up to three times more likely to experience domestic violence than are childless women (Mirlees-Black 1999). Once in an abusive relationship, women may have little autonomy over their fertility or sexuality. They may be pushed into pregnancies because their partners want a child, or a child of the 'right gender', or because the partners believe that burdening the

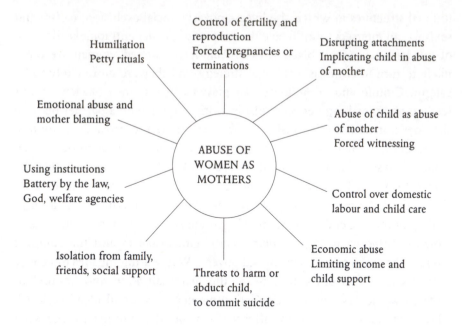

*Figure 2.1: Abusers' strategies for undermining mothers*

woman with several small children will keep her busy and prevent her from leaving ('keep a woman ill-shod and pregnant and she will never leave you'). Domestic violence often begins or increases during or after pregnancy (Hoff 1990; Mezey and Bewley 1997; Pahl 1985). Half the 65 women we interviewed had suffered violence during pregnancy. Some women say the violence is just 'business as usual' (Campbell *et al.* 1998a) but for many the abuse is clearly linked to the birth of a child. Reasons include:

- the man's sexual jealousy of the unborn child
- an immature personality unable to cope with competition for the woman's emotions or time
- the man's fear of the responsibilities the child will bring
- the man's attempts to cause an abortion (Schornstein 1997).

The transition to motherhood can be a delight and an excitement, but it is also a physical and emotional shock for many women (Oakley 1980). There are different expectations about parenting for men and women. Women may be overwhelmed or shocked at how mothering changes their lives, yet abusive partners often expect things to stay the same as before. The man's expectations can be very unreasonable and contradictory, setting her feelings about herself as 'mother' against his demands of her as 'lover':

> He called me names, fat this and fat that. When I had the baby, what a disgusting body I had, stretch marks and saggy tits... Oh he couldn't come near me. I'd made his stomach turn and made him physically sick to look at me. ('Brenda')

> He was very vicious and hurtful when I was pregnant and started putting on weight, he started saying, 'You slag, you're fat.' ('Angela')

The madonna/whore, mother/lover contradiction took a central place in violent men's undermining of new mothers' confidence. To guard their children from 'father deprivation', women are expected to provide emotionally or economically attached fathers for children. But beyond their presence in the birthing room, fathers are not widely expected to assume practical responsibilities for child care during a relationship. This leaves much of the negotiation of the father's role in parenting up to the mother, and abused women lack bargaining power. Violence resulted for some women during arguments about the time spent on caring for a new baby:

> After I had my son I suffered from post-natal depression and from the day I came out of hospital he just took everything out on me because he wasn't working. I had the baby and he just wouldn't help me and we were fighting and quarrelling and it just went from there. ('Janet')

Some mothers were expected to care adequately for the new baby but to do this without taking any extra time or attention from their partners. One man insisted that the woman stop breast feeding because he felt the baby took up too much of her time:

> He made me give up breast feeding after four weeks... He was jealous because I was breast feeding her and she was taking all my attention. ('Susan')

The isolation and burden of physical care may be increased through abuse in pregnancy, especially if the woman is forced to have a large family or has a low birthweight or sickly baby. An abuser may compete with and limit the time the woman spends on caring for herself during pregnancy or in looking after a newly born child.

Violence during pregnancy, especially sexual violence, can affect the attachment between mother and child. This may be especially the case if the child results from rape or a forced pregnancy. Some women we interviewed reported ambivalent feelings that also influenced how their children felt about them:

> With [my son] the first six months to a year, I didn't want to know him because he was his. I hated him, I really did hate him. And if I had somebody there to help me, I don't think none of that would have happened... We never bonded as much as we could. Even now, he's only just started giving cuddles and kisses, whereas before I had nothing like that. ('Charlotte')

Some women had more ambivalent feelings about their sons as they grew older and reminded them of the abuser. Some, like 'Charlotte', felt that having some social support might have helped them to cope better. To date, health care practitioners, especially in Europe and the UK, have not put very much effort into screening for women who might benefit from improved social support during pregnancy and childbirth. Routine questioning about domestic violence in ante-natal care would give health carers an opportunity to identify women living with domestic violence and strengthen the social support available to them (see Roberts, Hegarty and Feder 2005).

In Chapter 4 we review the research literature on children and domestic violence so we will not discuss this in depth here beyond noting, with reference to Figure 2.1, that men sometimes abuse children in order to further abuse the mother. Children may also be used by the violent parent to try to disrupt and undermine the relationship between mother and child. Involving children directly in the abuse of the mother can have a profound effect on a woman's feelings about the children and the children's attitudes towards the mother. One father made his seven-year-old son kick and punch his mother to 'teach her a lesson', despite the child's protestations and crying:

> He made them kick and punch me and they did because they were so frightened of him. [Son] kicked me, he punched me in the face. But, when he had done it his father told him he hadn't done it hard enough, and he was to go and put his shoes on and do it harder. ('Hilary')

Hilary's children later 'chose' to live with their father, not only because they feared him and feared leaving him because of his repeated threats and attempts to commit suicide, but because they lacked respect for the mother as a competent parent. Forced witnessing of the violence and involving children in the constant rain of criticism and name calling of the mothers was often reported and likewise undermined other women we interviewed:

He very often hit me in front of the children as well and he used to say 'Mummy's a waste of space. She has shit for brains'... [My daughter] was on my side, but at the time [my son] was growing up, he was two or three; I wouldn't say he was on his side but he got very confused about it all because I did everything for them, he didn't do anything... He used to sort of say, 'Well Mummy doesn't take you anywhere. I'm the only person that takes you to the seaside 'cos Mummy can't drive, Mummy's useless.' ('Belinda')

## Governance of the household

Gender entrapment results in women 'failing' in domestic labour and child care because abusers overload women with responsibilities as mothers while often severely limiting their financial, time and energy resource. Many incidents of abuse develop from arguments over money, housework or child care and the abuser's efforts to gain power and control over domestic labour (Dobash and Dobash 1998). It can be difficult for a woman to feed and clothe her children if her partner keeps her short of money:

When I had my first son, I begged the clothes for him. I never had new clothes for the children, just other people's castaways. And I've been so ashamed because I have even asked other children if they have some clothes for my babies. When I had my second one, my second son is now two weeks old, I ended up begging again... People started feeling sorry for me, they used to get bottles of milk for me. ('Ravinder')

The no-win situation for impoverished mothers is clear from this quote. Her partner would take all the family income, including any welfare payments. In the mother-blaming discourse where women's weaknesses and victimization take precedence, Ravinder has no choice apart from failure. She 'fails' as a mother by letting her children go hungry or she 'fails' as a member of her community by begging for food.

A mother's capacity and feeling of competence can be undermined by a violent partner's efforts to set impossible standards for household tasks and child care. The precise regimentation of household tasks and daily routines allows the abuser to monitor and restrict the woman's activities without necessarily having to maintain a constant physical presence. The film *Sleeping With The Enemy* illustrates this aspect of domestic violence well in the scene where the husband checks the kitchen cupboards and re-arranges the labels on the food tins so that they are all facing in the same direction. His daily ritual continues into the bathroom where the position of the towels on the towel rail and the method of folding them is monitored. He breezes through the house looking for any mistake or failing on his wife's part. To keep the peace, his wife complies with his demanding routines and obsessions and constantly tries to anticipate and monitor his moods and actions.

In *Sleeping With the Enemy*, the pursuit of order was a major feature of the man's abuse and control, and indeed many abusive men are known to write their partners lists that structure their daily routines and what they can and cannot do and think. But order is not a necessity for fuelling the relationship between abuser and abused of monitoring, checking and double guessing. Disorder and the lack of a predictable routine works in a similar way to restrict and control, and can do a lot to undermine a woman's confidence in her mothering:

> Whatever structure I made up in the house, he would just keep breaking it down to belittle me. ('Loretta')

No matter how carefully and precisely the woman monitors her partner's moods and organizes the domestic routines around his whims, she is set up to fail:

> It was always my fault, always, because I'd made him angry. It was always my fault, never his. He never apologized. ('Diane')

Her 'failure' allows him to blame her for the abuse happening and to complain that she is an incompetent mother, unable to cope with household chores, or to manage a budget and look after the children.

The 'traditional' heterosexual nuclear family is not the only context where violent men are able to confine and undermine women through housework and child care. Men exert similar control in extended family contexts by involving their mothers and female relatives in the woman abuse. Eight of the women we interviewed (five Asian, one Turkish, one white Irish and one white British traveller) lived in extended family households where responsibilities for housework and child care were divided among the women in the house. Charlotte, for instance, lived with her abusive partner and his extended traveller family. Her partner's control over her activities was greatly aided by his family's supervision:

> The minute he got me under his power, when I was living under the same roof as him, if I didn't wash up a cup instantly, he'd belt me over the head with something. His mum was the worst one, she used to come in and say 'Why is that washing up there, you should hit her for it.' ('Charlotte')

Women living with domestic violence in extended family households had low status positions in the home and were allocated the most menial domestic chores by the husband and his female relatives. Cooking food for the rest of the family was particularly likely to be tabooed by the husband's mother and sisters. Fara, a Turkish woman, was expected to do all the cleaning in a large house where the family were employed as domestic staff. She was not, however, permitted to take part in the cooking or eating of the communally prepared food. Her child and husband ate with the rest of the family, but Fara had to cook her food separately on a stove set up in a garage and eat there alone. Providing emotional care for children may be more difficult for a woman if the partner and his relatives isolate and undermine her within the broader family.

Isolating women as mothers from family, friends and external sources of emotional or economic support is a strategy many abusers use to make their partners' dependent solely upon them. Overburdening women with responsibility for child care and domestic labour, or restricting their movements so that they are rarely able to leave the home without children or without supervision, severely limits the options to escape from the abuse.

## Family and community ties that bind

Violent men often use a combination of force, fear, threat and blame to lock mothers and children in an abusive family. Getting out of the relationship safely with the children may be difficult. Some of the partners of the 65 women we interviewed used the children as ransom to prevent their leaving:

> He kept me a prisoner, he kept me hostage, and he could especially do that when I had my daughter, because I knew that if I left him I wouldn't be able to take my child with me… He's not afraid of the police, you couldn't put injunctions on my husband so he'd keep away, he doesn't care… I really wanted to get up and go but I couldn't, and not because I loved him and not because I was frightened of him, because I wouldn't have been able to take my child with me. ('Brenda')

> After he'd attacked me on the street, he always made sure he had one of the children…he knew that as long as he had one child I wouldn't leave him. ('Loretta')

In the NSPCC study, one father held a six-week-old baby over a first-floor balcony in order to try and prevent the mother from leaving after he had hit her. Threats to abduct or to snatch the children if she leaves, and threats to commit suicide, were also commonly used. In situations such as these, the decision to stay with the abuser may be seen as being the best option a woman has to prevent harm to her child.

The threat that they will bring dishonour upon the family and community if they leave or speak about the abuse is a problem faced by some women whose abusers use religion or cultural issues to maintain control:

> He sees me as a Western woman, not fit enough, not a good enough mother for his children… He doesn't see me as an Islamic person. I don't dress like a Muslim woman should… He's been telling people that I go to public houses, which I don't, that I mix with white men… One of his cousins even rang me up once and asked me how much I charged for the night. ('Kiranjit')

As with other faith communities, Christian beliefs can be used by perpetrators to justify domestic violence:

> Repeatedly I was told by my Methodist minister husband that it was my duty as a Christian to forgive. My children were told the same. I was also repeatedly told that as a Christian I had promised in my marriage vows 'For better, for worse'… Initially I strove as a Christian very committed to marriage to forgive but I came to see that although apparently there was a duty for me to forgive, there was no mention of repentance or sorrow on my husband's part or if there was, the words would prove to be insincere and the abuse would soon start again. (ex-wife of minister in Radford and Cappel 2003, p.29)

Beliefs about the permanence of marriage in many faith communities can be used, by perpetrator, family and the person who is the target of abuse, to prolong the relationship (Radford and Cappel 2003).

Leaving without the children and being prepared to cut off all contact with them was the only possible option some women saw for surviving themselves because having left before, they knew that the children would be used by the ex-partner to force their return. Threats to kill the children, harm the children, abduct them or inform social services that the mother was putting the children at risk were common tactics employed by the partners:

> I want to see them. But I'd never have dared go out of the house with them because I'd be scared of him. I don't want that risk being there all the time so I've had to cut myself off from them and not have any contact at all for myself, but it's hard. ('Alice')

Leaving the children with the abusive partner was a drastic step taken by three women we interviewed who feared for their lives and who knew from past experience that their partners would never let go. In Chapters 6 and 7, we show that women who leave their children find it very difficult to get safe contact and visitation. The violent ex-partner is almost guaranteed to use this as part of his post-separation strategy of 'battery by the law' (see Chapter 7).

## Conclusion

In this chapter, we have discussed how domestic violence affects women's experiences and their identities as mothers. We have argued that a key aspect of gender entrapment is the perpetrator's abuse of women as mothers, his overloading of her responsibilities in the relationship and as a parent, and the subsequent shifting of blame that results. It is important that professionals working with women who experience domestic violence challenge mother-blaming assumptions by drawing upon this knowledge of how violent men attempt to undermine women as mothers. In Chapter 3, we will look at the other side of the coin as regards gender entrapment – that is, women's coping mechanisms and their resistance.

# 3

# Resisting Mother Blaming

We argued in Chapter 1 that the individualization of responsibility for crime and victimization has provided a cultural and political context in which mother blaming can flourish and perpetrators 'disappear'. Women who are abused are sometimes seen by the police, child protection and the courts as responsible for their own victimization. Even some feminist interventions stress individual responsibilities by focusing on 'helping women to develop the personal resolve to stay out of an abusive relationship' (Nichols and Feltey 2003, p.785). We do not believe that there is one route that women follow when moving from 'victim' of domestic violence to 'survivor'. Not all women who have lived with domestic violence identify themselves as 'victims' or as 'survivors' because their experiences do not match the images that the terms 'victim' and 'survivor' of domestic violence invoke in contemporary cultural contexts. 'Victim' of domestic violence is associated with the term 'battered woman' so widely used in the US literature. This suggests the vision of severe, frequent physical assault verging on the lethal, and excludes the broader range of abusive, manipulative and controlling behaviour that domestic violence often includes. Women's experiences of domestic violence are very varied. Not all women who live with domestic violence are beaten daily by their partners, although research findings show that the violence may escalate in severity and frequency over the course of the relationship (Dobash and Dobash 1980). In our interviews with women, we heard that living with the threat of abusive behaviour may be constant for some women, but many also remember good times when the partner's behaviour rekindled their hope that things could change (Dominy and Radford 1996; Hester and Radford 1996a). The term 'battered woman' further invokes an image of the batterer as an all-powerful demon but the majority are ordinary men (Corvo and Johnson 2003), and, as others have noted, often also charming (Horley 2002). The term 'battered woman' is closely associated with the term 'battered babies' which was influential in shifting thinking about child abuse in the late 1960s (Parton 1990). Both suggest that 'real' child abuse or 'real' domestic violence involves brutal, anger-driven acts of cruelty perpetrated on passive victims. This ignores the complexities of an abusive relationship, the entrapment process and the ambiguous emotions that women may have about abusive partners. It also tends to distract awareness from any acts of resistance by the victim and does not leave much scope for the conceptualization of their own anger or fighting back.

Similarly, the term 'survivor' conjures up a heroic image of women who have lived through violence and all the consequences of abuse and emerged the other side as stronger people. This may match some women's experiences but overcoming domestic violence can be difficult if, as we show in Chapter 6, the ex-partner's abuse continues long after separation. As a result of continued abuse and living constantly in fear, only a minority of women we interviewed in the contact and inter-agency studies were in positions which could be described as being safe, so not all felt that they had yet 'survived'. Some of the women were still trying to come to terms with the disabling and devastating impact of the violence (Dominy and Radford 1996; Hester and Radford 1996a):

> I've got no memory. I can't think of a decent thing that has happened to me in my life and I'm only twenty-six... He's destroyed me. ('Brenda')

The term 'survivor' is useful because it draws attention to women's agency in breaking free from the abuse. Some women did feel they were stronger people due to the experience of having lived through and coped with the violence:

> It was a horrible experience but I've come through it. If I hadn't gone through it, if I hadn't met him, I'd be quite selfish and very intolerant of people, very dismissive of people with job problems. It has made me on the whole a much nicer person. I'm much stronger now. I've been through that and survived it reasonably intact. It's turned round to be quite positive. ('Val')

Being able to get through the abuse and cope with the financial, physical and emotional demands associated with rebuilding one's life must be a key aspect of overcoming domestic violence:

> Since I left I haven't looked back. The children have been really...they have improved a lot. I've changed completely...I can stand up for myself now...I've moved house which makes me feel better because it's mine...and everything I do in it is mine. I can manage brilliantly on my money...I've got

a job which I've never had before…I've got loads of friends now whereas before when I was with him I never had one. ('Alice')

As this quote shows, Alice was able to rebuild her friendships and her social support but she was still unsafe because of her ex-partner's ongoing harassment, so she had not as yet 'survived' the violence. The term 'survivor' can shift attention from the responsibilities of the broader community to stand by women and challenge the violence of men.

We have found it difficult to find terms that are more relevant to describe the range of experiences described by the women we interviewed in our contact and inter-agency studies (Dominy and Radford 1996; Hester and Radford 1996a). The language of victimization has become so invested with these cultural images of individual responsibility and blame that it is very difficult to find alternatives. In this book, we have avoided the terms 'battered woman' and 'victim' of domestic violence and have used instead the terms 'women who experience domestic violence' or 'women who live with abuse' because these terms refer more accurately to the range of abusive behaviour that is domestic violence. We have avoided the term 'survivor' as well and used instead the term 'overcoming domestic violence' because this term emphasizes the process of ending the violence and undoing the harmful consequences. It includes women's agency and the steps they take to cope with the abuse and to resist it by protecting their children and themselves. It also gives us more scope to emphasize the broader social responsibilities that exist to challenge the violence of men.

Positive and empowering practice and interventions with abused women require two basic elements:

1.  a commitment to safety, which means taking steps to stop the perpetrator's abusive behaviour;

2.  listening to women and building upon their coping strategies and protective behaviour.

In this chapter, we will look at some of the different ways that women cope with living with abuse and the efforts they make to protect and shield their children from the consequences.

## Coping with abuse

There are many things that women do in order to cope with the psychological and emotional consequences of living with a violent partner. Coping strategies will vary in relation to the nature and duration of the abusive behaviour, the specific strengths and vulnerabilities of the woman and her determination for self-preservation:

> [It went on for] about three years but I wasn't living in fear... I would always argue. It was almost like he was trying to break my spirit and I thought, you never will. You can hit me as much as you like, but you will never break my will or my spirit and make me totally submissive to you. I will always argue, I will always fight you back. ('Trish')

Although it happens, it is rare for the violence and abuse to be constant throughout a relationship. Sandra Horley, Director of the organization Refuge, in England, called her book about domestic violence *The Charm Syndrome* to draw attention to the fact that many women going through refuges describe their ex-partners as being 'charmers' (Horley 2002). The 'good times', or remembering the good times, can help women to get through times which are not so good. Occasional glimpses of the caring partner or father, or his making promises to change, can sustain women's hope that the relationship might improve. This can cause difficulties for children because mothers may be seen as clinging on to a hopeless relationship or colluding with the 'cover up' of domestic violence.

One way some women coped emotionally was to blank out the abuse and try to forget and pretend to the rest of the world, and to the children, that all was well:

> He hit me round the head really hard, he hit me so hard I must have passed out in the bathroom. And for a couple of weeks my whole head was swollen on the side...[my daughter] said, 'I heard you crying in the night'. And I sort of said, 'Oh don't worry, I'm just not very happy you know. ('Belinda')

Mental health professionals have found similar responses among adult survivors of child sexual abuse in the condition they call 'dissociation' (Herman 2001). It may be harder for a woman to talk to her children about their feelings if she is trying to cope herself by pretending that all is well.

Mentally trying to 'blank out' may be the only option when there is no physical way to avoid the abuse. Escaping from the violence in even the smallest way helped some women to maintain this 'front' of being okay so they could cope on a daily basis. Belinda, for example, told us how she pulled herself through the depression and suicidal feelings resulting from the violence. On one occasion, she gathered together tablets and a bottle of vodka but did not go through with her plan to kill herself because of the likely impact upon her children:

> I thought well I can't really put [my children] through that, so I decided that I'd do something else instead, and I locked myself up in the attic every evening and wrote short stories instead of committing suicide. ('Belinda')

Blanking out the abuse this way helped her cope for a short time and, because her partner had isolated her, the only refuge was within her own home, in the attic. The writing helped her to take stock of what had happened and to review how the violence had affected the children. This was a major factor in her, and in other women's, decisions to try to change things or to leave:

> Towards the end I was putting up with it because I was forgetting…or making myself forget…just to cope. Just pretending everything is fine but it wasn't. For my daughter's sake all I wanted was for her to have a relatively normal existence. So I'd kept on taking her to the park and the play group and acting as if everything was fine…and making myself laugh and joke. And in that way I was allowing it to go on. Then I started writing about it to make myself remember. ('Val')

## Protecting children

All the women we interviewed reported steps they had taken to protect their children and it would be inaccurate to say that they 'failed to protect'. When children were abused, women did intervene although sometimes it was impossible to prevent the child being attacked. Direct intervention to protect the child from an abusive partner takes courage:

> He did kick him [son] once and I hit him back with a chair so I got two black eyes and a bruised nose. ('Ros')

McGee (2000) similarly concluded that protecting children was uppermost in women's minds even when they were being attacked:

> He picked up a wooden coat hanger and started hitting me with it and I had Francis in my arms so I'm using my body to shield Francis to make sure that he couldn't hit Francis. (Judith, in McGee 2000, p.39)

Shielding children from the abuse by trying to manage the abuser's behaviour, or preventing the children from witnessing or overhearing the violence, were strategies women very commonly used. Finding a way to protect children from witnessing and living with domestic violence may not be straightforward. Managing the partner's behaviour may involve controlling the children, particularly if he starts rows over her 'poor' parenting and lack of control. In Chapter 4 we show that sometimes the mother's attempts to control a child can be abusive. Our own and other research suggests however that, where there is abuse of a child and the mother, the perpetrator of domestic violence is nearly always also the child abuser (Hester and Pearson 1998; Hester and Radford 1996a; McGee 2000).

It is difficult for a mother to protect a child from witnessing violence if forced witnessing is a fundamental part of the abuser's controlling behaviour. It may be particularly difficult for a woman to counteract an abuser's constant attempts to undermine and humiliate her in front of the children. Feelings of failure may be especially powerful for women who become unable to provide physical care as a result of the abuse, and for women who have been constantly undermined for being 'bad mothers'.

Many women tried to reassure their children when they were afraid. This finding is also supported by McGee's research (2000), as the following extract from her book illustrates:

> He came up the stairs, had me pinned against the bed, of course, the children were crying their eyes out. I'm just saying to them, 'Don't worry, don't worry', like, you know. (Amanda in McGee 2000, p.45)

Women's efforts to manage violence and create a sense of normality for children can make it more difficult for them to realize that their own well-being and the welfare of their children are inter-linked. Both McGee (2000) and Abrahams (1994) found that women who had coped on a daily basis with domestic violence were left feeling emotionally distant from their children. In our research, we found that during the relationship and especially after separation women tried to compensate for and to counteract their own feelings of distance and their partner's efforts to emotionally abuse and alienate the children:

> As a child James liked to come and sit and give you a cuddle and a kiss and if their dad was in the room he couldn't sit on your lap and give you a kiss because his dad used to say he was a nancy... 'You're turning out to be a nancy, you'll be a poof you will, keep sitting there giving your mum kisses and cuddles...' He had to be a boy you know. So I think that's why at times now I'm more overprotective of James... I like to sit him down and let him know that he's got a mum that wants to kiss him. ('Ros')

Women who compensated and tried to counteract the partner's emotionally distancing behaviour felt more able to repair relationships with their children after separation. It can be difficult to get this right though because freedom from the controlling family environment can leave the mother and children struggling over what the rules and boundaries of behaviour now are. Even women who were still involved in abusive contact mentioned great improvements in the levels of stress in the home. Freedom within the home and over daily routines, real choice about what to cook and what to do or not do, were positive changes a number of women mentioned:

> The first day that I left and started to get my own money, every day I would be thankful for something little like doing the shopping and being able to bring it home. And either not cooking meals because before I used to have a big fuss about whether I cooked or not – I went through a big stage where I didn't cook. I'd cook something ready prepared every night. It was only my kids there and no one complained at me, but now I cook occasionally and it's quite nice. I enjoy it but I needed a break. I had to rebel and stop it and now I realize that I like my meals home cooked every now and again so I make it. But it's not because anyone's telling me to…
>
> Now I wake up in the morning even though I've got two small children in some ways the day is still my own. I decide what I want to do… At first it was huge freedom. It was like having a big party all the time. But now I've got a bit more used to it and I realize it's normal and how abnormal everything else was. ('Zoe')

This finding reinforces the importance of supporting rather than undermining parenting of mothers who live with domestic violence, working positively with both the strengths and difficulties they face.

## Staying or leaving for the sake of the children

Concern about the well being of children plays a major part in women's decisions to stay or leave an abusive partner. Fear of losing the children should they leave keeps many women tied to violent men, particularly if they feel vulnerable to accusations about their mothering due to low self-esteem, depression, alcohol or substance dependency. Newly partnered women with insecure immigration status are also especially vulnerable because they lack welfare and citizenship rights (Gill and Sharma 2005). Women fear, understandably, that contact with social services may bring inappropriate intervention and judgement of them as 'unfit mothers':

> I went there thinking, if I kept my kids in that kind of relationship for seven years they are going to think I am a bad mother for it. ('Sally')

About one-third of the women we interviewed in the contact and inter-agency studies felt having children had made it more difficult for them to leave the violent partner. About the same number, a third, said they had left because of concerns about the children. The remainder had left in fear for their lives. Leaving was more difficult for practical reasons – where to go, how to cope financially. The emotional pressure put upon women as mothers – to provide a father for the children, to maintain the family unit and preserve links with the community – meant that some chose to stay for many years for the sake of their children:

> What made me leave the final time was when he attacked my baby…and my eldest son was having trouble at school, it was coming out in other areas of his life and I walked out and went to stay in the refuge for six weeks and he said he'd promise to behave himself and I had been brought up without a father. So he said, 'Oh you've got to give the children a chance, they need a father'. So I said, 'Alright, for the children's sake', and I spoke to the children and they said they wanted to go back…it was great for a couple of weeks. ('Loretta')

Staying for the sake of the children complicated the feelings of ambivalence and responsibility many women had towards their children. The older children, and boys in particular, put pressure on mothers to go back home sometimes by leaving their mothers to return to live with their fathers. Pressures from children to go home, coupled with feeling unable to cope alone, compounded women's feelings of failure, whether they left or returned.

Violence during pregnancy, especially increased abuse or violence after childbirth, was the turning point in the relationship for some of the women:

> He had me in hospital when I was eight weeks pregnant, I nearly had a miscarriage because he were hitting me and then he came round and said, 'Oh it won't happen again', and I was nearly 18 weeks pregnant, I nearly lost her again. I thought well I can't take any more so I left him. ('Ella')

A growing awareness of how the children were affected by the violence helped move women to thinking that they would be better off separating:

> When I first went to the refuge, I was pregnant with my second child and my son was about two and a half. I went because he was hitting my head against the wall…and it really distressed him [son]. He wouldn't attack any of the children but it really distressed my son. He kept on following us around from room to room and it got to the point where I'd be in the bedroom and I'd close the door and my son would say, 'Hide under the bed'…I had already

put myself through it before but I couldn't put my son through that fear that when he heard footsteps he would want to hide under the bed. ('Zoe')

For Madeleine, the turning point came when she realized that her partner's treatment of her son was the same as the abuse and humiliation he directed at her, so it was difficult to continue to think of him as being both a violent partner but worthwhile father figure. Madeleine's account of one episode involving her teenage son illustrates this disturbingly clearly. We have quoted her account of this episode in full because it illustrates so well not only this revelation on her part but also the intertwining of the abuse of the mother and child:

> He used to lay in bed and he used to whistle to the kids, 'Get out of bed and make me a cup of tea.' Right. So, L was lying there. He said, 'Go and make me some cheese on crackers.' Well, he always had cream cheese spread on his crackers. L was half asleep, went downstairs, cut him off like cheddar and put it on the crackers, and he cut it like this thick. And, like I say, with food he was spot on, you've got to have the butter in all four corners of the bread and that... So L took the crackers up. I'm laid in the bed and L used to have to stand at the end of the bed. He gave him the crackers and he looked at them and said, 'For two pins I would throw this at you.' And I thought, your stomach goes, 'Here we go again.' And poor L's standing there you know, I'm thinking, 'He's feeling the same as me.' And I said, 'Oh just eat them D. Stop going on. It's only bloody crackers.' And he sat there and he said, 'I'm not going to throw them at him.' He got out of bed and threw the plate so it went all over the floor. So L's picking it all up, putting all the cheese back on the crackers. And he grabbed him and smacked his [L's] head into the plate of food. And I mean, L was 15 then and like, the humiliation of it. So I got out of bed and just screamed at him, 'You're not going to do to him what you've done to me. Just leave him alone.' So he got on the bed and beat the living daylights out of me and he said to L, 'You tell your mother that if she opens her mouth again when I'm chastising my children she's had it.' So L's going, 'Mum, don't say anything.' And then he went to clout him again and I got up again because there was no way I was having that and he beat the shit out of me again. And then he gave L a clout and sent him to bed. Then he gets up in the morning, he's saying to L, 'Look what you've made me do to your mother. If you had cut the cheese properly on the cracker she wouldn't have got a hiding.' ... And then it was me, 'You made me give my son an extra hiding.' ('Madeleine')

Both mother and son saw they were in a 'no-win' situation. Walking on egg-shells to appease the abuser would no longer be enough. This episode cemented Madeleine's decision to leave to protect herself and the children. The awareness that her partner's contempt and maltreatment of her was the same as his contempt and maltreatment of her son was the key to her awareness that she was an abused mother rather than a mother who had failed.

It is clear from our research that women's decisions to stay or to leave were very much influenced by what they thought would be best for their children. The practical responsibility of having to care for children made separation easier for some women by opening access to services they might not have known about otherwise. Services accessible to mothers such as ante-natal and medical care were conduits to sources of help, especially for women who were isolated by the abuser's behaviour, lack of resources or language skills. This finding gives further support to the argument that good advocacy services in health care, especially for poor and ethnic minority women, can play a major role in improving the accessibility of services for women and children living with abuse (British Medical Association 1998).

## Conclusion

In Chapter 2, we argued that mothering plays a key role in the gender entrapment of battered women. The fundamental contradiction between woman as mother and woman as lover in the social construction of Western femininities contributes significantly to the gender entrapment of women mothering through domestic violence. Violent men often use children to abuse women, to undermine their sense of self-worth and femininity, their parenting and their relationships with children. It is equally important to acknowledge the part played by violence, mother blaming and gender entrapment in the poverty and social exclusion of women and children. In this chapter, we have tried to challenge conventional stereotypes of 'battered women' as 'victims' or 'survivors', arguing that few women who experience domestic violence identify with these terms.

Overcoming gender entrapment is a complex process in which women deal with domestic violence on a daily basis and try to protect and shield their children from abuse. These efforts can have contradictory consequences as the mother's efforts to shield a child and the child's efforts to protect the mother contribute to the conspiracy of silence about abuse. Training social workers, lawyers, shelter or refuge workers and health care professionals to talk to women frankly about domestic violence and mothering could provide many opportunities to move beyond the mother-blaming response but this will be ineffective if steps are not also taken to try to stop the violence.

Understanding how violent men may undermine women's parenting emotionally and materially may help professionals to respond more sensitively and build on women's own efforts to cope and be free from abuse, especially after separation. Our research lends further support to studies that have recommended an increase in routine questioning about domestic violence and safety planning, particularly in ante-natal, obstetric and early child care (British Medical Association 1998; Hester and Westmarland 2005). This would also enable professionals to identify children living with domestic violence at an early stage in their lives, to work in a supportive way with mothers and to challenge violent men. These issues will be revisited in Chapter 9.

# 4

# Domestic Violence and the Maltreatment of Children

As we began to outline in Chapter 2, children are a crucial part of the equation for women experiencing violence from male partners. It is important to recognize that women may decide to leave a violent relationship because they see their children affected by the violence, but that they may also decide to stay 'for the sake of the children' because the material circumstances are more advantageous for the children if they do so. Domestic violence perpetrators may draw the children into their abuse of the mother, or the children may also experience abuse directly from him. For mothers who have left violent men, children may enable the ex-partner to seek her out and to continue his abuse. In this chapter, we consider some of these aspects, examining in particular documented links between violence to mothers and the abuse of their children. In Chapter 5, we go on to discuss the impact on children of living in a context where their mother is being abused, as well as the implications for practice.

## Maltreatment and abuse of children in the context of domestic violence

In the UK as in North America, it was workers and volunteers in the women's refuges or shelters who first realized that children were also being affected by living in a context of domestic violence, and that there were overlaps between violence to mothers and maltreatment of their children. Shelters developed some of the earliest work with children on their experiences of living with domestic violence, which in the UK included the appointment in the 1980s of 'refuge children's workers' specifically responsible for children's welfare (Debbonnaire 1994; Hague *et al.* 2000). Recognition that children are affected in potentially detrimental ways by living with domestic violence has resulted in a wide range of programmes and interventions developed by domestic violence services and other organizations for children in Canada and the US, including group work and other programmes (Grusznski, Brink and Edleson *et al.* 1988; Hague *et al.* 2000). Support and programmes for children in the UK are more recent and draw on these North American and Canadian experiences (Hester and Pearson 1998; Hester and Westmarland 2005; Humphreys *et al.* 2000). Children's work in UK refuges or shelters continues to offer the main support for children who have lived with domestic violence, although other voluntary and state welfare agencies have also begun to work in this area (Hester and Westmarland 2005; Humphreys *et al.* 2000). Some of these approaches and related issues will be revisited in Chapter 9.

## The research on children and domestic violence

Since the 1980s, there has been an increasing body of research concerned with children and domestic violence. Much of the initial research was carried out in the US, Australia and Canada, but more recently a number of studies in the UK have echoed the findings from elsewhere. The research has both reflected and informed the often contrary developments in theory, policy and practice regarding domestic violence and child abuse (see Chapter 9 for further discussion). Research on domestic violence has tended to develop separately from child protection research, with evidence concerning the maltreatment or abuse of children in circumstances of domestic violence arising merely incidentally from either. A body of research examining co-occurrence of domestic violence and child maltreatment has now emerged, especially in North America (see Edleson 1999; Edleson, Daro and Pinderhughes 2004; Edleson *et al.* 2003), but still with relatively few studies in the UK (Cawson 2002; Hester and Pearson 1998; Mullender *et al.* 2002). Divorce and post-separation issues have also tended to be a separate area of research, not concerned or connected with the research on either child protection or domestic violence (Jaffe, Lemon and Poisson 2003; Jaffe, Poissan and Cunningham 2001).

The research on violence to women on the one hand and to children on the other has often employed a range of methodologies and relied on different theories. It has suffered from fragmentation into separate and seemingly disconnected 'violences' or abusive acts – not only 'domestic violence' and 'child maltreatment and abuse' but also physical violence, sexual assault, emotional abuse and neglect, with an often narrow conceptualization or definition of domestic violence as merely physical.

There are different research traditions in different countries, and this is apparent in the social research carried out in the US and the UK as regards domestic violence and children. In the US more resources have been committed to research coupled with more emphasis on development of treatment-oriented measures. This has led to a proliferation of large-scale quantitative studies in the US using comparative scales and inventories. At the same time, there has been a focus on incidence and prevalence statistics as well as attempts to correlate different forms of abuse including domestic violence and harm to children (Edleson 1999, 2001). Dobash and Dobash (1992) have described the US adherence to the social survey approach as a 'near fetish like commitment' where the weaknesses of such an approach are largely overlooked:

> While survey research certainly has its strengths, such as wide coverage… [it] is particularly poor at investigating complex behaviours, emotions and social processes such as those associated with violence, and its necessary brevity means it can rarely be used to explore the contexts associated with social behaviour. (p.276)

These weaknesses are exemplified, and continually replicated, by the widespread use in the US of versions of the Conflicts Tactics Scale in domestic violence research and now also research examining co-occurrence of domestic violence and child maltreatment (see Edleson 1999; Johnson 1998). There is a focus on the development of 'typologies' of both perpetrators and victims, a somewhat static approach where the shifts and changes in the way violence is applied and the dynamics of how it 'works' may be obscured. There are important implications for practice as, without understanding the complex domestic violence dynamics we have outlined in Chapter 2 and the varied and often hidden ways in which perpetrators use such violence against women and children, practice that is both limited and may further abusive experiences may result. Attempts to question and move beyond this narrow research base are however also evident, as exemplified by the use of other instruments and more detailed approaches (Edleson 2001; Edleson et al. 2004; Stark and Flitcraft 1996). The Canadian research has shown an even greater concern to move beyond this narrow base (Johnson 1998).

In the UK and the wider European context, there has been a stronger tradition of phenomenological and critical social research, also reflected in the research on domestic violence and to a lesser extent in that on child abuse

(Hester 2004). This has led to emphasis on examination and analysis of the dynamics and processes involved in abusive contexts via personal experience. Large-scale studies on domestic violence have tended to develop from this more detailed knowledge (e.g. Heiskanen and Piispa 1998; Kelly, Regan and Burton 1991; Lundgren *et al.* 2001). Studies have often included accounts of women who have experienced domestic violence, and examination of records from social services or health. Recently, there has been an increasing number of direct accounts from children who have lived in circumstances of domestic violence (McGee 2000; Mullender *et al.* 2003). There has also been a growing emphasis on multi-methodological approaches that provide more complex understandings of both domestic violence and the overlap between domestic violence and the abuse of children (Hester and Pearson 1998), as well as evaluations of projects concerning children and domestic abuse (Hester and Westmarland 2005).

## Linking domestic violence and child maltreatment and abuse

Despite the different methodologies in North America and the UK, it is possible to identify a number of consistent aspects across the studies that link violence to mothers and abuse of their children. In the late 1990s, one of us carried out a review of the UK research on domestic violence and children for the UK state department, the Department of Health (Hester *et al.* 2006). We found that, despite a variety of methodologies being employed, inconsistency between definitions, and lack of identification of gender of abusers or relationship to the abused (see Edleson 1999), looking across both UK and North American studies, it was nonetheless possible to identify a number of overarching themes. These were as follows:

- that the domestic violence perpetrator may also be directly – physically and/or sexually – abusive to the child
- that witnessing violence to their mothers may have an abusive and detrimental impact on the children concerned
- that the domestic violence perpetrators may abuse the child as part of their violence against women. (Hester *et al.* 2006, p.30)

This highlights the importance for practitioners of considering that violence to mothers is an indicator that child maltreatment and abuse may also be occurring; similarly, child maltreatment and abuse are indicators that domestic violence may be an issue. Questions about domestic violence and about child maltreatment need to be raised either way (Hester *et al.* 2006).

Some authors have cautioned that the research on children and domestic violence does not indicate any *causal* relationship between domestic violence and child maltreatment or abuse (Edleson 2001). Nonetheless, the existing and developing knowledge of co-occurrence of domestic violence and maltreatment of children already highlights that professionals need to be aware that men who are perpetrators of domestic violence are also likely to be abusing their children in some way, and that men who are intra-familial child abusers may also be abusing their wives or female partners. Such awareness allows disclosure and provision of support on an individual basis. The quest for 'causality' and ever more finely tuned 'typologies' may in this sense be counter-productive and possibly undermine the ability of professionals to provide sensitive responses and support tailored to specific individual need.

Edleson (1995), overviewing American studies, suggests that, in 32 per cent to 53 per cent of all families where women are being physically beaten by their partners, the children are also the victims of direct physical abuse by the same perpetrator. Other key findings have been that domestic violence provides the most common context for child abuse (e.g. Stark and Flitcraft 1988), that the greater the severity of the abuse of the mother the greater the severity of children's maltreatment and abuse (e.g. Bowker, Arbitell and McFerron 1988), and that men are not only the most frequent domestic violence perpetrators but are also more likely to be abusing their children in this context (Ross 1996; Stark and Flitcraft 1988).

## Linking domestic violence and maltreatment and abuse of children – knowledge from UK domestic violence and child protection studies

Research in the UK focusing on domestic violence, in particular on women's experiences, has consistently revealed a link between domestic violence and physical and/or sexual abuse of children. It has also shown that the majority of children living in circumstances of domestic violence witness the violence and abusive behaviour to their mothers (see Table 4.1). The studies have included interviews with women in shelters or refuges and children's organizations as well as random community samples. The earliest of these studies, by Levine (1975) of 50 families with 117 children seen in a general medical practice, found that the 'children who observed their parents in violent conflict' were in danger of physical harm and/or detrimentally affected by observing the violence.

## Table 4.1: Links between domestic violence and child abuse in domestic violence and child protection studies

(Note: This table provides a selective rather than a comprehensive or systematic listing of the existing research.)

| Study | Sample | Links between domestic violence and abuse of children |
|---|---|---|
| *Domestic violence studies* | | |
| Levine (1975) | Surveyed 50 families with 117 children seen in a general medical practice. | The 'children who observed their parents in violent conflict' were in danger of physical harm and/or detrimentally affected by observing the violence. |
| Dobash and Dobash (1984) | Interviewed 109 mothers from shelters or refuges. | Over half (58%) of their children had been present when there was violence to the women from male partners. |
| Abrahams (1994) | Questionnaire survey of 108 mothers from NCHs (National Children's Homes) family centres who had experienced domestic violence. | At least 27% of the children were said to be physically abused by the domestic violence perpetrator (who was usually the father). Almost three-quarters (73%) of the children witnessed violent assaults on their mothers, and almost two-thirds (62%) overheard violent incidents. |
| Hester and Radford (1996a) the 'contact study' | Study of child contact cases in England and Denmark in circumstances of domestic violence, including interviews with 53 mothers in England (see Chapter 1). | 21 (40%) of mothers reported that their children had been physically and/or sexually abused by fathers. |

| | Community survey of domestic violence with a random sample of 484 women, 171 service providers and 23 interviews with abused women including 12 about mothering (see Chapter 1). | Half the mothers (6 out of 12) reported that their children had been physically and/or sexually abused by fathers. |
|---|---|---|
| Dominy and Radford (1996) The 'inter-agency study' | | |
| **Child protection studies** | | |
| Maynard (1985) | Examination of 103 social services case files. | One in three (33%) mentioned domestic violence. |
| Hooper (1992) | Study of 15 mothers of sexually abused children. | In 9 out of 11 instances involving the father (or father figure) as the abuser, the woman had also experienced physical, verbal and/or sexual abuse from the same perpetrator. |
| Radford and Gill (2004) | 41% of the 362 children on the West Sussex child protection register in 2002 were living with domestic violence. | For 149 of these children domestic violence was identified as a significant risk factor. |
| Cleaver and Freeman (1995) | Detailed study of 30 families undergoing the early stages of child abuse enquiries. | 12 of the cases (nearly 50%) also involved domestic violence. |
| Gibbons, Conroy and Bell (1995) | Examination of 1888 referrals to social services with child protection concerns. | In 27% cases domestic violence was also recorded. |
| Farmer and Owen (1995) | Study of outcomes of child protection practice with 44 sample cases. | 52% of sample cases involved domestic violence. |
| Forman (1995) | Interviews with a self-selected sample of 20 mothers of sexually abused children with social services involvement. | All the mothers had also experienced violence or abuse from the same men who abused their child, mainly the natural fathers. |

*Continued on next page*

*Table 4.1 cont.*

| Study | Sample | Links between domestic violence and abuse of children |
|---|---|---|
| *Child protection studies cont.* | | |
| Brandon and Lewis (1996) | Examination of significant harm of children (that is, maltreatment and neglect) with 54 children in the background sample and 51 children in intensive interview sample. | Nearly half (21 out of 54) of children in the background sample and more than half (28 out of 51) of children in the intensive interview sample had witnessed domestic violence. |
| Humphreys (2000) | Study of 32 Coventry social services child protection cases. | In nearly one-third of cases (11 out of 32 ) women were also reported to have severe injuries as a result of incidents of domestic violence. |
| Hester and Pearson (1998) The 'NSPCC study' | Examination of 111 NSPCC case files accepted for service. | In at least a third of cases accepted for service, domestic violence was also an issue. This rose to nearly two-thirds (62%) after the team included a more detailed focus on domestic violence in their work. |
| Farmer and Pollock (1998) | Study of substitute care for sexually abused and abusing children, including case file sample of 250 newly looked after children and more detailed follow-up sample of 40 sexually abused and/or abusing young people in care. | Two in five children (39%) in the case file sample had lived in families where there was violence between their parents – mainly violence by the man to the mother. This rose to over half (55%) in the more detailed follow-up sample. |
| Cawson (2002) | Retrospective survey on childhood experiences with a national random probability sample of 2869 young people aged 18–24. | 26% of the young adults reported physical abuse by parents or carers during childhood. For 5% this violence was constant or frequent. Moreover, where they had experienced neglect, in 88% of cases there was co-occurrence of violence between their parents or carers; and domestic violence was reported by 80% of young adults who had experienced serious physical abuse. |

In the 1980s, Dobash and Dobash (1984) interviewed 109 mothers from shelters or refuges, and found that over half (58%) of their children had been present when there was violence to the women from male partners. In the 1990s, there have been further studies, including one by National Children's Homes (NCH) Action for Children (Abrahams 1994), involving a questionnaire survey of 108 mothers from NCH's family centres who had experienced domestic violence. At least 27 per cent of the children were said to be physically abused by the domestic violence perpetrator (who was usually the father). Almost three-quarters (73%) of the children witnessed violent assaults on their mothers, and almost two-thirds (62%) overheard violent incidents.

In our contact study (Hester and Radford 1996a), 21 of the 53 women interviewed in England reported that their children had been physically and/or sexually abused by fathers, with a further 6 out of 12 in our inter-agency study (42% overall). In 11 instances, there was social services involvement with regard to abuse of the children by fathers. Consistent with other research, we found that the more severe and frequent the violence to the mother, the more likely it was that the children would also be abused. The greater the isolation of the mother and children from family, friends and community, the more likely it was that the abuse would also be potentially lethal. The abuse children suffered tended, however, to be less life threatening than the violence their mothers experienced. Men who were violent to partners during pregnancy more frequently employed potentially lethal violence or its threat towards the children. In at least one instance, the man's violence led to a child being born prematurely:

> As a result of his violence [my daughter] was born a month prematurely. I delivered her myself at home. ('Hilary')

Life-threatening violence to the children was more common after separation.

In the UK in the late 1980s, a number of cases involving child deaths highlighted the importance of domestic violence as a context for child abuse, although not generally acknowledged at the time. Domestic violence was found to be an important feature in the highly publicized death of Maria Colwell at the hands of her father in 1974. Similarly, in the backgrounds to the fatal abuse of five-year-old Sukina Hammond by her father, and of three-year-old Toni Dales by her stepfather, was the ongoing violence and abuse from these men to the children's mothers (Bridge Child Care Consultancy 1991; National Children's Bureau 1993; O'Hara 1994; and see also the report on the death of Kimberley Carlile [London Borough of Greenwich 1987]). Yet in these, and many other cases where children have been killed, the significance of violence to the mothers as an indicator of potential risk to the children was neither understood nor acknowledged by the professionals who intervened (James 1994; O'Hara 1994). As O'Hara explains:

> In both [the Dales and Hammond] cases the professionals involved with the children suspected that they were being physically abused and knew that their mothers were being subjected to violence by their partners, and in both cases there was a failure to appreciate the danger to the children represented by the men concerned. (O'Hara 1994, p.59)

It was only during the 1990s that the links between domestic violence and child abuse emerged in the public and social work debates in the UK.

Child protection studies have probably provided the largest body of research in the UK to indicate, if incidentally, that domestic violence is an important feature in the background of children who have been subject to abuse or risk of harm. There are certain limitations to the use of child protection data, in particular that it provides narrow 'clinical' samples which are unlikely to be representative of the population as a whole (Hester *et al.* 2006). Only a small proportion of incidents of child maltreatment and abuse come to the attention of welfare agencies, with under-reporting in relation to middle-class sectors of the population and over-representation of ethnic minorities (Hooper 1995; Kelly *et al.* 1991). There has, since the 1980s, been a tendency in the UK to equate child abuse with sexual abuse, and research involving child protection has thus provided samples of children whose 'presenting issue' is considered sexual abuse. Nonetheless, from the child protection studies, it is apparent that domestic violence is often a significant and consistent feature, no matter what the form of maltreatment and abuse a child is deemed to have suffered, whether physical, sexual or emotional (see Table 4.1).

The studies indicate that, in instances of child maltreatment and abuse, between a fifth (20%) and more than three-quarters (88%) of the children were also living in circumstances of domestic violence (see Table 4.1). The more detailed or in-depth the studies, involving interviews as well as detailed surveys and/or case analysis, the more likely they have been to find that domestic violence is also an issue.

Our NSPCC study (Hester and Pearson 1998) focused specifically on domestic violence in child abuse cases referred to the NSPCC which has a statutory child protection role and carries out therapeutic or recovery work with children who have been abused. The study highlighted the direct links between sexual abuse of children and living in a context of domestic violence.

Moreover, mothers and children were found to be most likely to be abused by the same perpetrator, who was usually the children's natural father. Most of the 111 cases accepted for service by the NSPCC team during this period involved sexual abuse as the main concern (77%), with the children also experiencing a range of other abusive behaviours including physical and emotional abuse. Social services were involved in some way in 61 per cent of the cases. Significantly, over half the sexual abuse cases also involved domestic violence (almost exclusively male to female violence). With regard to the perpetrator, in just over half (53%) of the general sample, the child sexual abusers were the children's fathers or father figures. This rose to over two-thirds (69%) in instances where domestic violence was also identified. In other words, fathers or father figures were even more likely than other men to be sexually abusive to their children where these same men were also violent and abusive to the mothers.

From the child protection studies, a number of key themes emerged of importance for practitioners:

- Children with the worst outcomes were most likely to have mothers who were being abused by male partners, yet social work and other practitioners ignored the domestic violence and/or domestic violence perpetrators (Farmer and Owen 1995).

- Asking specifically about domestic violence massively increased the number of disclosures (Hester and Pearson 1998; and see Hester and Westmarland 2005).

- Mothers and children were most likely to be abused by the same perpetrator, usually the child's natural father (Forman 1995; Hester and Pearson 1998; Hooper 1992).

## Living with and witnessing violence

Alongside the work examining direct physical and sexual abuse of children in contexts of domestic violence, attention has also been focused on the experiences of children living in such contexts but who might not be being 'directly' abused. Those cases involving the direct abuse of children are more likely to come to the attention of child protection services, but there is also a growing recognition that living with or growing up in an atmosphere of violence can have detrimental effects on the children concerned. Despite differences in research methods and in measuring instruments used, in their review of the literature on children witnessing domestic violence, Kolbo, Blakely and Engleman (1996) conclude that there is clear evidence from all these studies to suggest that witnessing violence can have a negative effect on children's emotional and behavioural development.

In a sense, this development parallels the studies concerning women's experiences of domestic violence, where physical violence from male partners was initially focused on, but with an increasing recognition that the psychological effects of living with the fear and threat of possible violence often has a greater impact on the women concerned (see Hester *et al.* 2006). In recognition of the potential impact on children of witnessing domestic violence, during the 1990s a number of local authorities in the UK defined witnessing domestic violence as maltreatment and abuse of children – for instance, Strathclyde Regional Council Social Services Department (Hague *et al.* 1996). As was previously the case in the US (e.g. Minn. State Ann. 626.556), this has more recently been reflected in English law, with a clause to the effect that witnessing violence may be harmful to a child included in the Adoption and Children Act 2002 (section 120, implemented from January 2005). It should be noted that in Minnesota the initial legislation was repealed because it resulted in a large increase in maltreatment cases without the services to match. Edleson (2001) has argued that exposure of children to adult domestic violence should not automatically be defined as maltreatment under the law because only some children concerned are at great risk of harm and should therefore be referred to the child protection system, with the majority of the children and their families being offered assessments and services outside the criminal justice system. As will be discussed further in Chapter 9, the UK child protection system already uses a 'welfare' approach rather than prosecuting abusive parents. In the UK system, being deemed at risk of significant harm not only leads to registration within the child protection system but has also been used as a route where services are more likely to be offered to support the family in parenting. Having to use registration in this way has also been subject to criticism (DH 1995). Edleson's suggestion, enabling rationalizing (or rationing) of services, was thus in many respects already in place in the UK system by the later 1990s via the differential emphasis on children being 'in need' or 'in need of protection', with the latter linked more often with resourcing (Hester *et al.* 2006; and see Chapter 9), with services most likely to follow registration. The Department of Health (1999) has suggested that it will often be appropriate to regard children in situations of domestic violence as 'children in need' (DH 1999, para 6.37), although this becomes somewhat irrelevant if services are not available. Another problem likely to arise from the new English legislation is that mothers will continue to be blamed for 'failing to protect' their children, rather than male perpetrators being brought to account.

In the UK context, Brandon and Lewis (1996) examined significant harm in relation to children who had witnessed domestic violence (see Table 4.1). ('Significant harm' is the term used in Section 1 of the Children Act 1989 to refer to the level of harm to a child that will invoke a child protection response.) Fifty-four children were in a 'background sample' and 51 in an 'intensive interview sample' which included information from parents, teachers and from some of the children themselves. Overall, approximately half (49%) the children from each sample group had witnessed domestic violence. About half (28 out of 51) of the intensive interview sample 'warranted inclusion as cases of harm or potential harm from domestic violence' (p.36). Brandon and Lewis (1996) conclude that the abusive consequences of witnessing domestic violence generally need to be recognized by social workers and other professionals:

> the evidence points to the possibility that the cumulative harm from witnessing violence will affect the child's emotional and mental health in future relationships... Until professions recognize that when the child sees violence at home there is a likelihood of significant harm, it will not be possible to act to prevent long-term damage. (p.41)

'Witnessing' domestic violence may suggest that the child is present in the room or location when an incident takes place. However, children can 'witness' domestic violence in a number of ways that extend beyond direct observation of violent and abusive acts to their mothers or other carers. Where children do not directly witness the violence or abuse, they might still overhear incidents or in other ways be aware that violence or abuse has occurred. Hughes (1992) found that in 90 per cent of cases children are in the same or the next room when domestic violence takes place. In our NSPCC study (Hester and Pearson 1998), the case files were found to contain several examples of children having witnessed attacks of physical violence towards their mothers. This included instances of children seeing their mothers being stabbed in the head or being attacked with a knife, or attempts at strangulation. As indicated in Table 4.1, in the NCH Action for Children study (Abrahams 1994), 73 per cent of the children had directly witnessed violent assaults on their mothers, including 10 per cent of the children whose mothers had been sexually abused or assaulted by violent partners in front of them, nearly two-thirds (62%) had overheard violent incidents, and about half

(52%) saw the injuries resulting from domestic violence (p.30). Children interviewed in the study recounted some of these incidents:

> He would come in and rip my mother's clothes off. He tried to strangle her, just to beat her up like… We were always watching it… He used to tell us to get back to bed…' (Child, in Abrahams 1994, p.31)

> A lot of times I just heard it from the bedroom, and once (my sister) and I heard it, and we were just crying our eyes out for my Mum, you know, she just sounded so desperate downstairs…crying and screaming. (Child, in Abrahams 1994, pp.31–32)

> It was depressing. My mother was always on edge, scurrying around… And I was frightened as well, every time he was there, thinking, 'Oh, what's he going to do today? Is he going to knife her or what?' (Child, in Abrahams 1994, p.33)

It also has to be recognized that children do not witness violence to their mothers incidentally. Abusive fathers may actively involve the child in the violence to the mother by making him/her watch the abuse. In our NSPCC study (Hester and Pearson 1998), for example, a father locked the children in the room with him, while he physically attacked their mother, thus forcing the children to witness the abuse.

Much of the research has focused on the witnessing by children of physical violence to mothers; however McGee (1996 and 2000) points out that witnessing other ongoing abusive behaviour is at least as important because 'many children may not directly witness the physical assaults but will be exposed to other forms of violence and abuse directed at their mother' (McGee 1996, p.5). In interviews with children and young people, a 12-year-old girl told her:

> I've never seen Dad hit her, but I've seen him get very angry and like once when Mum was really ill, she had to be taken to hospital in fact, he said, 'No, just leave her, leave her'. And then I was the one who had to phone the doctor. (p.6)

Not seeing directly what is happening to their mothers, children do not know what is happening or what to do about it, and this increases their feelings of powerlessness and trauma (McGee 2000).

Children are also likely to witness violence to their mothers. in relation to contact with violent fathers, where mothers are involved in hand-overs (see Chapter 6).

## Violence to children and mothers – part of the same abuse

As we outlined in Chapter 2 and recently in relation to witnessing abuse of mothers, violence to children and violence to women are not only likely to be part of the same abusive incident but aspects of the same pattern of controlling behaviour by the perpetrator. Men's abuse of their children and partners may be difficult to separate into discrete categories of 'child maltreatment and abuse' and 'domestic violence' where the intention of the perpetrator is that the violence or abuse of the child will have a directly abusive impact on the woman (Hester *et al.* 2006; Kelly 1996). Both Hooper (1992) and Forman (1995) argue, on the basis of their studies concerning mothers of sexually abused children, that the sexual abuse of the children could be seen as connected with the domestic violence or abuse of the mothers. The violence to the mothers also served to distance them as a source of support for the children, so that the men could more easily continue their sexual abuse. Hooper, for instance, found that the violence to mothers often preceded the sexual abuse of the children and usually continued alongside it, such that the man's abuse of the children was also directly intended to be abusive of his partner:

> Children were used by violent men both to extend means of control over their mothers (for example, by battering or verbally undermining women in the presence of children as well as by sexually abusive behaviour) and to extend their domain of control to someone with less power to resist. (Hooper 1992, p.355)

Our NSPCC study (Hester and Pearson 1998) provides examples where abuse of the woman and the child(ren) by the same man was so closely inter-connected that they were simultaneous expressions of both domestic violence and child abuse. This included an example where the father held a six-week-old baby over a first-floor balcony in order to try and prevent the mother from leaving after he had hit her. In another example, the mother was unable to intervene to protect her children from the man's physical abuse of them because she was too frightened of the repercussions of this for herself. In our contact study (Hester and Radford 1996a), there were also instances where the children had become implicated in the violence against their mothers through being forced to further the father's abuse – for example, the father who made his seven-year-old son kick and punch his mother (see Chapter 2). Some of the men used the children to force the women to stay within the relationship, with one father ensuring he always had one of the children with him as he knew his partner would not leave him without them

(Hester and Radford 1996a, Chapter 2; and see similar incidences in Malos and Hague 1993, Chapter 3).

Children may also be hurt in trying to protect the mother, or mothers hurt in attempting to protect the child. In McGee's interviews with mothers and children, mothers frequently talked of intervening to protect a child and then being beaten themselves. For instance:

> Yeah, because he took everything out on her, everything was always her fault, I always sided with her, constant beatings, most of it was all about Mona [daughter]. Because he would treat her in a way, and I would intervene and say no, and then he would start on me, but at least it took the heat off her. ('June' in McGee 2000, p.46)

In our contact and inter-agency studies (Dominy and Radford 1996; Hester and Radford 1996a), half of the abusive incidents on children reported by mothers were part of the same violent incident as that involving the mother (Table 4.1 and Chapter 1).

Children were hurt 'incidentally' as bystanders or witnesses to the abuse of the mother:

> He threw this chair at me and Katie was in the way and it caught her on the side of the face. ('Alice')

In some cases, the physical assault of the child followed an assault on the mother:

> As she got bigger and was walking around when he used to beat me up, she used to stand in the corner and shake and scream and then he'd start on her. ('Bea')

Perpetrators would also aim assaults at both mother and child, with instances of violence during pregnancy or attempts to kill the mother and children by setting fire to the house.

## Conclusion

Together, the material concerning children and domestic violence in this chapter, and the discussion of domestic violence and mothering in the previous chapter, indicate the situations – involving fear and danger – that provide the backdrop for future decisions and arrangements regarding children's ongoing contact with fathers post-separation of the parents. Practitioners need to be aware of the complex and often hidden or 'normalized' ways in which domestic violence perpetrators actively continue their power and control over women and children. They need to consider the possibility of maltreatment and abuse to children where mothers are being abused and, vice versa, that mothers may be being abused where there is evidence of child maltreatment and abuse. Without asking about domestic violence, it may be unlikely that practitioners will know that domestic violence is an issue for the women and children concerned.

# 5

# Children Living with Domestic Violence – Impacts and Resilience

As argued in Chapter 4, violence to mothers is an important indicator of risk to children. Children are likely to be abused by the same perpetrator as the mother, usually the child's natural father. Research has also indicated that children may be adversely affected by living with domestic violence, although it is becoming clear that different children react in different ways and that the relationship between the violence and the effect it has on a child can be both complex and multi-faceted (Peled and Davis 1995; Saunders *et al.* 1995). A range of personal and contextual factors can influence the extent of the impact (Kelly 1996). These 'mediating variables' are often referred to as 'protective' or 'vulnerability' (or 'risk') factors in that they can improve or accentuate the child's response to the violence. However, we still lack detail about how such factors influence children's perceptions and reactions, both in the short and longer term (Jaffe *et al.* 2003; Moore *et al.* 1990). In this chapter, we begin by examining some of the impacts on children of living with domestic violence to their mothers, going on to discuss how practitioners may help to enhance children's 'protective' factors.

## The impact on children of living with domestic violence

As indicated in Chapter 4, there is a growing recognition that living with or growing up in an atmosphere of domestic violence can have detrimental effects on the children concerned, with such children exhibiting more 'adjustment difficulties' than children from non-violent homes (Jaffe *et al.* 1990; Kolbo *et al.* 1996; Rossman 2001). The length and frequency of exposure to violence appears to have a direct impact on the severity of children's reactions (Hershorn and Rosenbaum 1985; Jouriles *et al.* 1987). Some clinicians and researchers have linked the trauma of experiencing and witnessing domestic violence with the impact exemplified by post-traumatic stress disorder (PTSD). Some of the resultant manifestations are numbness and detachment with withdrawal, disturbed sleep (possibly with recurrent dreams), impaired concentration and memory, hyper-alertness and 'jumpiness', and experiencing of 'flashbacks' (Harris Hendriks *et al.* 1993; Jaffe *et al.* 1990). These reactions may become apparent much later than the traumatic event (Jaffe *et al.* 1990).

McGee (2000), from her interviews with children and mothers about their experiences of domestic violence, echoes the general findings that living with domestic violence may impact widely on children's emotions, relationships, achievements and behaviour leading to:

> Fear, powerlessness, depression or sadness, impaired social relations, impacts on the child's identity, impacts on extended family relationships and their relationship with their mother, effects on educational achievement and anger, very often displayed as aggressive behaviour. The child's relationship with the father or father figure is also clearly affected by the violence to the mother. (McGee 2000, p.69)

It should be noted that, until the mid 1980s, many professionals within the field of psychiatry took the view that children of all ages react only to a 'mild' or 'transient' degree to situations of overwhelming stress, such as that created by living in a context of domestic violence (see Harris Hendriks *et al.* 1993). This view has now been superseded by the findings from research into domestic violence and children. By direct contrast, research from the neuro-psychology field has indicated that the impact on children, and especially very young children, of living with the trauma of violence and abuse may have a longer term impact on neural development (Radford 2004a; Rossman 2001). It is argued that this may result in heightened sensitivity to trauma, and consequently more reactive, impulsive and violent behaviour. Whether neural pathways are affected in this way in the shorter or longer term is still open to debate; however, there is no doubt that children are affected in many negative ways by experiencing domestic violence. A further problem for children, which we began to discuss in Chapter 2, is that the impact of violence on the mother may undermine attachment between her and the child, creating further vulnerabilities for the child concerned.

Some earlier research had suggested that children who were abused physically and/or sexually, and had witnessed domestic violence, showed most distress (Davis and Carlson 1987; Hughes 1988; Hughes *et al.* 1989). Hughes and her colleagues (1989) refer to this as children being 'doubly abused'. Others have suggested that children react more to the stress experienced by their mothers than to the violence itself (Hershorn and Rosenbaum 1985; Thoburn *et al.* 1995; Wolfe *et al.* 1985). In our research, we have found that it is the fear of their mothers dying as a result of the violence that has a particularly profound effect on the children concerned. One child talked about how, as a consequence, it seemed even more frightening to talk openly about what had happened to her mother than about the abuse she herself had experienced, in case the father resumed his abuse of the mother (Hester and Pearson 1998).

In the following sections, we outline some of the key issues arising from the impact of domestic violence on children (see Figure 5.1). In our contact study, the majority of children were reported to be adversely affected by witnessing violence to their mothers, and to be suffering harm which included nightmares, bed wetting, anxiety, aggression and delayed development. In the NSPCC study, there were examples of children 'acting out' with knives, or (by contrast) becoming withdrawn and silent, or expressing fear of being beaten up 'like mummy' or that their father 'could kill them all', and having nightmares, being scared of the dark, frightened of loud noises, having temper tantrums, being 'uncontrollable' and doing self-harm. In research with mothers at the children's charity Barnardos (Hester and Scott 2000, 'the

*Figure 5.1: Impacts on children of living with domestic violence*

Barnardos study') children had also suffered developmental delays, and some were using the controlling and abusive behaviours they had experienced at home. Children (even within the same family) were often affected in quite different ways.

### Young children and the minimizing of impact

Children remembered violence even though their mothers did not realize that they had been aware of it. In one instance, an older child recounted the violence she had witnessed as a much younger child (aged two or three) and, in another, a five-year-old-daughter recounted:

> unprompted memories from the past of abuse…that she observed and which…[mother] remembers but never thought [daughter] had seen. (Hester and Pearson 1998 p.33)

This replicates the findings from Jaffe, Wolfe and Wilson (1990) from North America that even very young children are aware of violence occurring around them and can be adversely affected, although they cannot necessarily make sense of it at the time.

Children below the age of two years were more often described by mothers and professionals as not likely to have been affected by the domestic violence (Hester and Radford 1996a). They were deemed to have been shielded by the mother from witnessing the abuse. However, mothers may under-estimate the impact of the violence on their children, believing that children are unaware of the violence – for instance, if they are not present or if the violence occurs at night. Some mothers feel that they have managed to protect their children from the worst of the violence when, in fact, the children were fully aware of what was happening. The findings from our NSPCC study (Hester and Pearson 1998) also confirm that children tend to keep silent about what they know or have observed, and will only disclose this when they are in some way given permission to do so. Both Abrahams (1994) and McGee (2000) suggest that mothers who thought there had been no impact on their children because they were still babies at the time of the violence might have been over-optimistic in their assessment.

### Educational achievement and developmental delays

From our studies, it was apparent that children's development and schooling are detrimentally affected by living with domestic violence. In a few instances, however, the children achieved very highly and this was also a part of their reaction to and ability to cope in relation to the abuse. A number of children were reported to be delayed developmentally, with this becoming more apparent for some when violence was happening at home. Delayed speech was an especially obvious indicator of the child being affected by living with domestic violence:

> he saw a lot of violence and his speech is very delayed. ('Davina' – contact study)

> she had nightmares and everything after [witnessing violent assault on mother]… My eldest daughter is affected very, very badly and I mean, she's tried to settle into senior school this year and her teacher's been really worried because of the effect this is having on her. ('Laura' – contact study)

One of the pre-school children in the Barnardos study, Robbie, was obviously affected when his mother was being abused at home (Hester and Scott 2000). His speech was badly affected and he would also become quiet and clingy. This was even more apparent at the time of domestic violence incidents:

> when [Robbie] is in Nursery, if there's any emotional turmoil at home, i.e. if [stepfather] is on the phone, then he exhibits certain behaviour that usually reflect what's going on. So, I mean just last week he was withdrawn, he was unusually affectionate, which he isn't usually, to a point where I think he was quite clingy, and he was gazing into the middle distance, you know, not concentrating. But his speech has always been like a particular sort of yardstick. (Social worker – Barnardos study)

> There are very serious concerns really by us and by Nursery about his development and his developmental delay particularly around his speech and his communication… (Health visitor – Barnardos study)

However Jamie, Robbie's younger brother, was not so obviously affected by living with domestic violence. Yet, exhibiting no obvious effect does not mean that a child is not affected, although it may be more difficult to ascertain that there is a problem:

> They're very different children. They're different ages, and I think they respond very differently at the moment to what's going on. We don't know what [Jamie's] going to be like when he's a bit older, but certainly at the moment he's an easygoing little fella. And so, really there's nothing to indicate at the moment from the younger one. (Social worker – Barnardos study)

Other children's schoolwork was affected by living with domestic violence, something that became especially obvious with regard to one of the children once he and the mother had left the violent father:

> we'd moved into a new house and we'd settled down, and the school that my children had been attending they couldn't believe the difference in the children. They said, 'Oh it's like having a new child in the classroom', he's confident, he's this, he's that, he's really getting on with his school work. ('Loretta' – contact study)

### Bedwetting because of fright

Whether witnessing violence to mothers and/or experiencing violence and abuse themselves, many of the children became extremely frightened of their fathers. One child started bedwetting at age five years due to his father's violence, and only stopped again once he felt safe at the shelter or refuge:

> He never ever wetted the bed as a baby, but from the age of five and a half he did wet the bed and then when we were first in the refuge when we first left their dad, he wet the bed about three times. But then we got him over that fear because there was the worker there. ('Roz' – contact study)

Another child, no longer living with the father, wet herself from fear when they met in the street:

> A couple of times we've been coming home and he's been outside the department store on the other side...and [daughter] started screaming really, really loudly... Actually she did actually wet herself that particular time. She's not wet herself since she was two years old. That's how scared she is. ('Monica' – contact study)

### Impact on health

For some children, their father's violence had a profound effect on their health as in the case of one little boy in our contact study whose severe eczema was clearly related to his father's abusive behaviour:

> The last year that we were together, in the end he had to have his legs bandaged up they were in such a state, it was horrible. Since his father left it has gone completely, so I think perhaps that was why. ('Mary' – contact study)

*Acting out and social interaction*

Nigel, a boy in the Barnardos study, was (like Robbie) also described by practitioners we interviewed as being badly affected in his communication with others. His speech was not delayed as in Robbie's case, but he had particular problems relating to and mixing with other children, and often acted violently towards them:

> [Nigel] doesn't concentrate. (Social worker – Barnardos study)

> His development in the gross motor and the speech and the fine motor skills were fine, but his social development was delayed, as in his mixing and being able to socialize with other children, members of his family. *That* was always a concern. (Health visitor – Barnardos study)

And he acted violently to the other children at school, scratching their faces:

> His first few weeks [at school] he could not, he just could *not* keep his hands to himself. And it was scratching. And for a couple of weeks almost every child had a gouge down their face that [Nigel] had put there in his first few days… And so we had to do a lot of work all the time with him then, constantly reminding him of what the expectations were and that he would have more friends if he didn't touch…attack every body. But things are a lot better in that respect. But when all else fails he will lash out. (Teacher – Barnardos study)

There were also concerns that Nigel was copying his father's abusive behaviour:

> And sometimes the way he talks to [his mum] is very much copying the adult dominance and verbal abuse really. So he obviously has taken note of what he's seen and uses it. (Health visitor – Barnardos study)

Again, the younger child in the family, Nigel's sister Susan, appeared to be affected less obviously by living with domestic violence: '[Susan] is a very bright and bubbly child…she's inquisitive…she's demanding, you know, bright.' (Social worker – Barnardos study)

One of the older school-age children, Albert, who was described by his teacher as 'a very bright boy' was not affected in his communication skills by living in circumstances of domestic violence, and indeed he was very articulate. Instead, he appeared to cope with the 'out of control' experience of living with violence by being quite controlling in his relations with others. This behaviour would become especially obvious at times of renewed domestic violence against his mother:

You know he liked to control the other children, you know, in a nice way, but he likes to have sort of be in charge and because he is very articulate, they let him get away with it really. And when they don't go along with what he wants them to do, he gets very upset. Tearful, and sort of sulky and with-drawn... [Following incident] And I noticed he was trying to take control quite a lot at that time, and then when it didn't work out he'd get very upset. (Teacher – Barnardos study)

## Is there a cycle of abuse?

Some of these examples of the impacts on children of living with domestic violence would suggest that children are growing up to replicate aspects of the behaviour they themselves were subject to. In other words, that there is a cycle of abuse whereby patterns of abusive behaviour are handed down the generations from parent to child. The idea of a 'cycle of abuse' is often used by practitioners and in the media, although there has been much discussion over the years about whether or not there is evidence to show that such a 'cycle' actually exists. The research evidence is more contradictory and on the whole does not unequivocally support the claim that there is an inter-generational 'cycle' of abuse. Individuals who grow up with domestic violence do not all end up in violent relationships, and adults in violent relationships did not necessarily experience domestic violence or other abuse as children. Resilience research further breaks down the myths that children who have lived with domestic violence will inevitably have abuse in their relationships as adults. Around a third of children who live with abuse grow up determined never to themselves abuse others, and they succeed in this goal (Blum 1998).

The idea of a 'cycle of abuse' also suggests a direct and causal relationship between childhood and adult abuse, which is too simplistic an understanding of the impact of abuse and the many factors, both individual and societal, which influence that impact. However, as outlined in this and earlier chapters, we know from studies of child maltreatment and abuse (whether physical, sexual or psychological), and from studies of children living with domestic violence, that the impact of these abusive experiences varies greatly between individual children. The impact is mediated by many different 'resilience' variables including self-esteem, the timing of incidents, the child's ability to attach meaning to and make sense of events, and the child's relationships with others (Rutter 1988). It has to be recognized that there is no uniform response to living with domestic violence or other forms of abuse (see Hester *et al.* 2006).

## Resilience and children's coping and survival strategies

While living with domestic violence can undoubtedly have adverse effects on children, it is important to recognize that children are not merely passive bystanders to events around them, but will act and make choices in highly individualized ways in order to cope with and improve their situation (Hester *et al.* 2006; Mullender *et al.* 2002). Research evidence suggests that many children will develop complex strategies of survival in order to deal with the stress and adversity they are experiencing, dependent to a certain extent on each child's behavioural and emotional development or resilience (Jaffe *et al.* 1990). It is estimated that between 55 per cent and 65 per cent of children who live with domestic violence appear to be 'resilient' and show no adverse effects (Hughes, Graham-Bernham and Gruber 2001).

In what follows, we first outline what resilience is about. We then go on to look at some of the coping strategies used by children living with domestic violence, and in particular protection and the mediating influence of mothers. The chapter ends with a discussion of ways in which professionals have enabled children to build on their resilience and ways of coping.

### *Resilience*

There has been an interest in children's resilience (or 'protective factors') since the 1980s. Garmezy and Rutter (1988) began looking at resilience when they found that about a quarter of children living with drug-addicted or severely depressed mothers were seemingly healthy and capable. At first, they concluded they had made mistakes and then refocused their research to look at coping skills. Others have more recently gone on to apply the idea of resilience within the context of domestic violence (Hughes *et al.* 2001; Mullender *et al.* 2002). Mullender *et al.* (2002), from their research on children's perspectives on domestic violence, found that two aspects, both involving children's active participation, were especially crucial to children's ability to cope:

- being listened to and taken seriously as participants in the domestic violence situation

- being able to be actively involved in finding solutions and helping to make decisions (Mullender *et al.* 2002, p.121).

Generally, the research to date echoes this finding and indicates the different ways in which these aspects may act as 'protective factors' and provide resilience for children with different personalities and circumstances. These aspects will now be detailed. It should also be recognized, however, as

Mullender *et al.* (2002) point out, that many of these aspects are also precisely those undermined by living with domestic violence:

***Characteristics of the child*** – Children's ability to cope with abuse, neglect and other adversity is linked to their age, gender and individual personality (Cleaver, Unell and Aldgate 1999). The child's cognitive ability and cognitive flexibility can influence his/her ability to adapt to changing circumstances. Albert, in the earlier example, had learnt by the age of 12 to cope with the abuse at home by controlling his environment, particularly his peers, through his verbal prowess.

***Self-esteem*** – children with higher self-esteem, e.g. children who excel at school, may gain approval for their abilities and strengths and will often cope better. Believing in oneself and recognizing one's strengths can help a child to partly mitigate the emotional and psychological consequences of abuse. Albert is again a useful example in this regard. The teachers described him as 'very, very bright', and he excelled at school work as well as at football. Albert tried hard to minimize and thus contain his experiences of seeing his mother abused. His involvement in activities outside home – in particular, football – played a central role in his ability to do so, and the teachers would use this to build his self-esteem:

> You know he tends to sort of shrug things off, as if you know, this isn't really anything different from what's happening. You can see him sort of trying to move himself on from it rather than dwell on it. 'Cos he can get quite upset by things… Things in his life that are very important are things like going to football. And he's always talking about how good he is at football and how long he's been doing it and things like in sharing times, you know when they want to bring something and talk about it. I mean today he's shown us his goalie gloves, because those are the most important things in his life. He's had them for three years and he can work out how many goals he's let through and how many he's saved you know, and that seems to be where he gets his self-esteem from, being good in goal. (Teacher – Barnardos study)

***A supportive caring relationship with a non-abusive parent or carer*** – being able to talk to a non-abusive parent about the abuse or living with domestic violence can be helpful. Mothers may find it difficult to talk to children about the violence, believing this to be protective and/or because they are unsure how to do this (McGee 2000). We have found many mothers do their utmost to protect children from witnessing the violence despite the reality that most

children are aware of its occurrence and can describe episodes they have witnessed without their parents' knowledge (Chapter 3; Hester and Pearson
1998; Hoff 1990; Jaffe *et al.* 1990). Thus, although children generally want to
talk about their experiences of domestic violence, they are often unable to do
so with their mothers (McGee 2000). This may in turn have its own impact on
children's well-being and feelings about the relationship.

In our NSPCC study, a child's angry behaviour was resolved positively in
therapy by enabling the mother to talk with the child about the domestic
violence from the father that they had both experienced:

> [Mother] was having difficulties with her little girl's behaviour…she's very
> angry because her father wouldn't let her have any of her belongings ever.
> He's still got all her toys – everything. And Mum kept saying things like, but
> I'm sure you're too big for them. And she started kicking and biting and
> scratching her mum again. And I said, well maybe she sees you as the strong
> person now and forgets what it was like – so she doesn't see why you can't go
> and get them, so just talk to her about what it [the experience of the domestic
> violence] was like… So just explore that anger with her and tell her, you
> know, Mummy is angry too, Mummy can't have any of her things. So that's
> what she did the next time she got angry and, yes, it worked, and the little
> girl kind of had a long conversation with her mother about [it]. (Hester and
> Pearson 1998)

*Other sources of support* – the most resilient people do not generally cope
alone. Children who are 'stress-resilient' are more likely to have people to
whom they can turn for emotional support (neighbours, friends, peers,
teachers, etc.) and are good at getting support from others around them
(Kashani and Allan 1998). Albert's experience at school is a good example of
this (see earlier). In another instance, a teacher had developed a 'diary
approach' to support a child who was facing great difficulties at home due to
the father's abuse of the mother and the father's new girlfriend: the teacher
had established an individual 'disclosure mechanism':

> There's a family that I visit that the children are very affected. The oldest one
> goes to school and reports to the teacher. Most mornings he has a little diary
> that he fills in himself, that's just for him. And if he wants to show it to the
> teacher he can. And it's often around 'I want to kill myself. My father beat my
> mom up last night.' Or, 'He went to see his girlfriend and he hit his girl-
> friend. He shouts at me. He plays rough with me. He hurts me.' (Health
> visitor – Barnardos study)

*A range of problem solving approaches (Rutter 1985)* – the two main strategies children use are to try to control the problem by intervening or 'managing' the parent's behaviour, or trying to control their own distress or fear. Features linked with children's resilience or coping may differ according to the adverse circumstances. Rossman and Rosenberg (1992) suggest that children's beliefs that they can intervene in situations beyond their control, such as living with domestic violence, can heighten their vulnerability and stress, whereas children's beliefs that they can manage their own emotions may buffer stress. Children who intervene to stop parental violence tend to show more negative outcomes than children who hide and try to protect themselves (see also later section on 'protecting').

*Hope or faith can be important* – the book *Once in a House on Fire* by Andrea Ashworth (1998) provides an example of how hope for the future can help children to cope. The African-American researcher David Miller talks about how, as a child living with violence, he used to follow the path of the power lines hoping that one day they would lead him to a better place (Blum 1998).

*There is no set time for finding coping skills or resilience* – children tend to do better if they develop coping skills in the first ten years of their lives, but the ability to turn around is always there.

*The level of security and chaos in the child's life will have an effect* – research by Kashani and Allan (1998) supports this conclusion. In their population survey, 16.7 per cent of 'well-adjusted' adolescents had lived with domestic violence. These adolescents differed from their maladjusted peers in a number of respects. Their families had greater financial security. They were less likely to have moved home on a number of occasions. They had better social support systems and were more likely to describe their parents as 'caring'.

The application of these 'measures' of resilience are by no means straightforward. A child's observable reactions may not necessarily match their emotional state. There is a need to employ broader measurements of resilience to take into account the possible mismatch between a child's symptoms – or lack of symptoms – and his/her emotional state. There is also a lack of research into how children fare in the longer term. Children may do better or worse with the passage of time. Some researchers suggest that, during childhood, children cope with or survive abuse and neglect, but it is not until they reach adolescence that they begin to transcend the problems they faced as children and start to rebuild themselves. Distinctions need to be drawn between children coping with, compensating for and overcoming abuse or neglect.

### Coping Strategies

Our contact research highlighted the various and often complex strategies for survival which children of all ages adopted in order to reduce the violence to themselves and/or their mothers (Hester and Radford 1996a). The survival strategies adopted can be diverse and may appear contradictory. For instance, some children choose various reactive and pro-active methods to try and keep their mother and/or siblings safe, including physical intervention, withholding information, or getting help from neighbours or from formal organizations.

Some children feel so concerned for their mother's safety that they want to protect her all the time. In such cases, children might refuse to go to school or feign illness so that they can stay at home with their mother. Some children's coping strategies will change over time. One young woman (aged 17) interviewed in Hague *et al.*'s study (1996), who had lived with violence over a ten-year period, explained how her initial protective way of coping had changed to staying away:

> At first I was: I wouldn't leave my mam. Wouldn't leave her anywhere. I was round her all the time. And then, when I was about 14, I used to just stay out all the time…I used to stay at my real dad's, at my sister's. At my boyfriend's. Anywhere. Anywhere I could just to get out of the house. (p.98)

Even young children can show very complex patterns of protective intervention, such as trying to mediate between their parents or acting as a distraction to bring the violence to an end. These protective responses may become more frequent than distressed responses as children get older. (Cummings, Zahn-Waxler and Radke-Yarrow 1984). Many of the children in Abrahams' (1994) study were younger children (the average age was 6.7 years), but almost a third (31%) were reported by mothers as being protective towards them, which for 22 per cent of the children also included physically intervening to try and stop the violence:

> My mother sounded so desperate downstairs…crying and screaming…so we went downstairs with our tennis racquets and started hitting him. (Child, in Abrahams 1994, p.37)

For some children, this desire to protect their mothers also includes fantasizing about killing the violent partner and plans for revenge (Weinehall 1997).

For others, these fantasies might be a way of dealing with the guilt, shame and fear that they feel concerning their own perceived inability/failure to protect their mothers.

Other children protect their mothers in less direct ways – for example, by learning that their presence in the room will bring the violence to an end. There were a number of examples of this in our contact study. For instance, a six-year-old boy came to realize that his father's violence would stop if he entered the room, and he consequently adopted this as his protective strategy:

> my son, he actually stood on the top of the stairs listening every time my husband raised his voice, he was getting very upset and he knew that something was going on. And he actually told me himself that he knew that his dad was going to do something to me because he said 'I'm listening up the stairs. You think I'm asleep but I'm not.' …he started coming down on a regular basis, when we had rows, arguments, because he knew that he could prevent his dad from hitting me. Because he knew that he would not hit me in front of the children. ('Nina' – contact study)

Other children were said to have intervened by screaming at their fathers to stop hitting their mothers or to stop threatening them with knives or other weapons:

> On one occasion I'd gone out and when I came back I found her standing by the back gate with a big stick ready to defend me if he attacked me. ('Rowena' – contact study)

> I was unconscious…and I just opened my eyes and I could see her standing in the doorway, she was crying, 'Don't hurt Mummy, please don't hurt Mummy.' ('Hilary' – contact study)

> the older one had had enough by then, I mean she went mad, and the little one tried to go for him. 'You touch my mum again and I'll hit you one.' I don't know why [partner] was so scared of the little one. I still don't know to this day why he was frightened of her. It was really strange. But the older one went running out into the garden screaming. ('Monica' – contact study)

Children may also try to protect their mothers by gaining practical help and information for them. Many children contacting ChildLine (the UK-wide children's telephone helpline) about domestic violence, for instance, requested details of women's shelters or refuges to pass on to their mothers and said that they encouraged their mothers to leave (Epstein and Keep 1995).

Another way some children protect their mothers is by taking on responsibilities in the home, such as child care for younger siblings and household chores, in the hope that this will help to keep the peace. If this fails, then they will provide support for other members of the family after a violent episode and/or they may try to placate their fathers (Jaffe *et al.* 1990). This assumption of adult responsibilities can lead to children becoming 'parental children', which can be burdensome, and may also prevent children from asking their mother for help (Epstein and Keep 1995). After a woman has left a violent partner, this sense of responsibility to protect their mother might be expressed by some children as wanting to live with their father. Though apparently contradictory, this might appear to the child to be the best strategy to adopt to keep their mother safe from further violence. It may also serve to allow children to act as caretakers for their fathers in those situations where the father has made threats to commit suicide if the mother and/or children leave (McGee 2000). Other children, especially older children, may adopt strategies aimed at self-protection, including presenting an external front of fearlessness in order to hide the fear and anxiety that lies beneath the surface (Grusznski *et al.* 1988).

Children are likely to believe that they are somehow responsible for the violence, and indeed are aware that violence can stem from arguments over child care, children's behaviour or discipline, or from resentment about the amount of time women devote to their children (Grusznski *et al.* 1988; Hilton 1992). This sense that they have in some way 'caused' the violence can lead children to attempt to modify their behaviour (by being quiet or 'perfect' – this latter might include excelling at school) in the hope that this will prevent an episode of violence, thereby protecting their mother. Even babies are reported to sense that changing their behaviour can have an effect on what happens in their environment. A children's worker in Hague *et al.*'s (1996) refuge survey, for instance, noted how living with domestic violence could lead to babies being withdrawn and 'unnaturally' quiet:

> this baby just sits there and stays stumm, because it has learned that is the best coping tactic. (p.43)

Similarly, one of the mothers in the same survey reported that her two older children had immediately taken to sleeping all through the night, as though this was a way of ensuring that 'nothing bad would happen' (p.43). In our Barnardos study, some of the younger children had also adopted a coping strategy, which appeared to be to switch off completely, and to go completely blank. For one of them, who had recently started school, the teacher was considering how to help him develop this in a more positive and productive direction:

> at least he has got that strategy. And it's trying to use that, in a sort of a pro-ductive way really isn't it? … Only I haven't got that far yet as to 'perhaps instead might like to go to a quiet place in the room and read quietly, or look at a book or draw or something like that and calm yourself down.' It hasn't got that far yet. (Teacher – Barnardos study)

Other children decide that their optimum chance of survival might lie in siding with the father, including sometimes joining in with the abuse of the mother (Hilton 1992). This identification with the abuser might also provide some children with a sense of control in a frightening situation (Grusznski *et al.* 1988), and might include expressions of anger and aggression towards their mother, either for her (perceived) failure to protect them and/or because they mirror the abuser's habit of blaming her for causing the violence (Abrahams 1994; Saunders *et al.* 1995).

## Conclusion

The effects children might experience in circumstances of domestic violence can include a wide range of (often contrary) behavioural, physical and psycho-logical effects, which may have either short-term and/or long-term effects. For instance:

- being protective of mother and/or siblings by physically intervening, withholding information, getting help, etc.
- advanced maturity and sense of responsibility
- aggression/anger to mother and/or others (including other adults and siblings)
- emotional confusion in relation to parents
- poor social skills
- highly developed social skills
- ability to negotiate difficult situations (see Hester *et al.* 2006 for further information).

It is important that practitioners work with children to enhance their individ-ual resilience and coping strategies, and to enable them to change coping strategies that may have negative outcomes to those that are more likely to be positive.

Mediating factors that will influence the resilience and coping strategies of individual children might include any of the following (not in any rank order): age, race, socio-economic status, gender, culture, religion, the emotional/physical development of the child, issues concerning disability or sexuality, the child's role and position in the family, relationship with her/his parent(s) and/or relationship with siblings, the child's relationships outside the family (including with peers, other adults and other family members), the degree of maternal stress, the frequency and form of the violence, and the length of exposure to the violence (Hester *et al.* 2006).

# 6

# Re-asserting Power and Control in Child Visitation and Contact

Post-separation violence is a key aspect of gender entrapment. Violent men who (may) have been removed and encouraged to stay away by the police and the criminal courts have then been enticed back into their families through visitation and contact arrangements for children. Keeping in contact with violent fathers is almost always viewed as being in a child's best interests (Hester and Harne 1999; Mason 1999). This thinking, which was never based upon much evidence about what was actually best for children, has put separated women and their children at greater risk of abuse and harassment.

In this chapter, we critically review the assumption that children must have contact with fathers, and we show the negative consequences of contact between children and violent men. We present case study material to illustrate how contact can be used by violent ex-partners as a direct route to abuse of the mother, to abuse the mother by abusing the child or to control, harass and impoverish the mother through repeated court appearances and litigation abuse. In this chapter, we argue that it is vitally important that mothers feel safe about visitation and contact arrangements because it is in the child's best interests to have peace at home. In Chapter 7 we will develop the analysis of gender entrapment and litigation abuse by reviewing the law's approach to child custody, visitation and contact.

*A note about language*

In America, the term 'child visitation' is commonly used to refer to a child's contact with the non-resident parent after separation or divorce. In England the term 'contact' is the norm. 'Contact' is used in the English courts to refer to direct contact visits, meaning the child's and non-resident parent's meetings or visits; indirect contact, meaning communication between the parent and child by phone, letter, email, etc., or a passing of information from parent to child, sometimes through a third party. We mostly use the term 'contact' in this chapter because it covers the broader range of possible activities and communications between a child and a non-resident parent. We do not discuss in any great detail the notion of 'custody' of children. The term 'custody' is an outdated concept with roots in the patriarchal structure of 19th-century family law where father's rights were dominant. The term ambiguously suggests ownership/imprisonment and guardianship of children. In the family law in England and more recently Canada, Australia and New Zealand, the term custody has been removed and replaced with language that stresses more what parents should do, rather than what their rights to ownership are regards their children. The language is deemed to better reflect the needs of children, emphasizing 'parental responsibilities' or making 'parenting orders' about where a child will live and how parents will provide care and support, including the contact between parents and child after the separation. In this chapter, it is the everyday living arrangements of children that we want to explore.

## Divorce, separation and the welfare of children

In the past 10 years, there has been bitter dispute about father's rights and the care of children after divorce and separation. In the UK, fathers have staged elaborate protests outside courts, judges' homes, in Parliament and in public places such as motorways. In 2003, a group of aggrieved fathers dressed up in Santa Claus costumes and staged a protest outside the London High Court. One father dressed up as Spiderman and spent three days suspended from a crane over a main road disrupting traffic. Another father spent several years staging a range of protests that included a tractor rally outside a leading judge's home and threatening to blow up a bridge on a main road. The British Prime Minister, Tony Blair, was 'bombed' while making a speech to government when father's rights protesters threw flour-filled condoms at him from the Palace of Westminster visitors' gallery. The media in Britain has mostly responded with gushing sympathy towards these fathers who are portrayed as being driven to drastic action because of being unjustly deprived of their 'rights' to see their children by bitter child-snatching mothers in cahoots with the family courts. Recently, sympathies have swung and the leader of Fathers 4 Justice, Matt O'Connor, disassociated himself from the group following publicity over a plan to kidnap the Prime Minister's five-year-old son. Nonetheless, the voices of the children and mothers in these disputes have been buried under the rhetoric about co-parenting and have not been heard. Indeed, mothers who do speak out risk being held in contempt of court if they have ongoing cases, because in English courts a cloak of secrecy covers family law proceedings. This overwhelming emphasis on fathers' rights misdirects attention from the rights and welfare of children and what actually happens after parents separate.

A recent overview of research findings on children and parental separation in England and Wales drew the following conclusions:

- Over 80 per cent of children live with their mothers after their parents separate.

- Only a minority of parents, one out of every ten, go to court to sort out their post-separation child care.

- Where parents do go to court, between 75 per cent and 86 per cent of the applicants are fathers.

- In the cases that go to court, the majority of children, 69 per cent, have regular (at least monthly) contact with their fathers.

- Most parents, resident parents and non-resident parents are satisfied with the arrangements for their children's residence and contact. There is little evidence to support the view that most mothers are against fathers having contact with their children.

- The majority of children want to preserve contact with both parents (Hunt and Roberts 2004).

In most cases therefore, contact is what parents and children want to happen and they sort it out themselves. There is no evidence from surveys of court cases that mothers frequently try to exclude fathers from contact with their children after separation (Smart, Neale and Wade 2001). Even women who have experienced domestic violence often support contact between the father and child (Hester and Radford 1996a; Radford *et al.* 1999). Children, as the following extract suggests, may want to continue to see their fathers after separation because, despite the abuse, they remain emotionally attached to them:

> I like to see him now we're away from him. Mum doesn't see him though. Thank goodness... He doesn't admit it [the abuse] or even think about it, I don't think. He thinks he's the king...I think he's an arsehole most of the time – excuse me – but I do kind of love him too because he's my father. So I don't want to lose touch with him. (Sharon, in Mullender *et al.* 2003, p.48)

Difficulties arise if parents do not agree and women who experience domestic violence and/or their children are likely to be at risk of further abuse.

## Children's welfare and parental contact

Article 9 of the United Nations Convention on the Rights of the Child (not ratified by the US government) sets out the principle that a child has the right to know and have contact with her/his parents and family. Contact is thus a right of the child, providing this is in the child's best interests. However, surprisingly little is known generally about what post-separation parental contact arrangements are best for children. Various authors have recently brought together and reviewed the literature on divorce and the welfare of children with the literature on domestic violence and children. The general research on child contact is limited, the findings are inconsistent, few studies consider the longer term outcome of contact on the child's welfare and it should be noted that most ignore domestic violence (Jaffe, Lemon and Poisson 2003; Hunt and Roberts 2004). It should not be assumed that it is always in a child's best interests to have contact with both parents and their families. There is no research that shows children benefit in the longer term from having regular face-to-face meetings with a violent parent whose behaviour has not been challenged. We show later in this chapter that contact with a violent parent is potentially very risky for children and for their mothers.

We do know that contact that starts well continues to go well and often improves with time. Conversely, contact that starts with problems tends to deteriorate as time goes by (Trinder, Beek and Connolly 2002). Children benefit most from contact that is conflict free (Rodgers and Prior 1998). There is a strong link between the distress of the child and parental distress (Bream and Buchanan 2003) so the health of the main carer after separation is an important factor for courts to address. Post-separation contact between a child and a non-resident parent needs proactive efforts to make it work, and there is no magic formula to enable this to happen although good communication between the parents is essential (Smart *et al.* 2001).

Claire Sturge and Danya Glaser, two experts who gave testimony in the important case *Re L, V, M & H (Contact: Domestic Violence)* [2000] 2 FLR 334 before the English Court of Appeal in 2000, reviewed psychiatric knowledge about children and parental contact. Sturge and Glaser claim that courts need to think about the *purpose* of contact and how a child might benefit from it. Continued contact with the non-resident parent can serve the following purposes for children:

- It could help the child to maintain a meaningful and beneficial relationship, or help to build one for an infant.

- It could provide the foundation for the child's healthy emotional growth by giving the child the message that s/he is important to the parent and is loved.

- It could allow the child, parent and family to share knowledge and information about their origins and histories. This can help a child develop a positive self-identity or open the door to further contact later if the child wants it.

- It could allow the child and parent to repair a problematic relationship.

- It could give the child an opportunity for 'reality testing', allowing him/her to balance reality against fantasy or idealization against denigration.

- It could give the child the opportunity to sever a broken relationship and to say goodbye. (See Sturge and Glaser 2000)

Where there has been violence or abuse, it is much more difficult to establish worthwhile visiting contact for the child although direct visiting contact may not be the only option to consider. Other forms of indirect contact and passing on information may be appropriate for a child's needs. Sturge and Glaser recommended that courts start by understanding that *direct visiting contact is less likely to work and benefit the child if there has been domestic violence*. The child is much less likely to have had a beneficial relationship with the violent parent and it is difficult to repair the relationship if the child and mother fear the father and he is unwilling to accept his responsibility to change.

## Research on contact and domestic violence

The rest of this chapter takes a detailed look at women's experiences of child visitation and contact, drawing on the authors' qualitative research with 53 women, the contact study (Hester and Radford 1996a) and the contact arrangements made by the 130 recently separated parents surveyed for the AMICA (Aid for Mothers Involved in Contact Applications) study (see Radford *et al.* 1999). The women's accounts of contact difficulties pre-date some major changes in family courts, especially since the year 2000 (discussed in Chapter 8), but they are discussed in detail because, in our opinion, they illustrate so well the abuser's efforts to use the opportunity of contact with children to sustain power and control over his ex-partner and children.

Between them, the 53 women interviewed in the contact study had 120 children and the 130 parents (129 women and 1 man) surveyed for the AMICA study had 215 children. The ages of the children ranged from two weeks old to adulthood but in both studies most children were below the age of 11 years (80% of the children in the AMICA study were six years or under). All the parents had separated from violent partners, having suffered frequent and severe domestic violence. In 40% to 55% of the families, children had also been physically and/or sexually abused by the violent partner before separation (40 per cent of the mothers reported their partners' physical or sexual abuse of a child in the contact study; 55 per cent of the children in the AMICA study were said to have been physically abused by the partner). In keeping with other research findings on post-separation contact (Hunt and Roberts 2004), in the majority of cases the children lived with their mothers after separation and the fathers became non-resident parents.

## Establishing contact

Apart from the few so in fear of their lives that they had tried to disappear, most women found the fathers asked for contact with children soon after the separation. The majority of women interviewed in the contact study, and 35 per cent surveyed in the AMICA research, at first saw some value in maintaining contact between fathers and children and made great efforts to ensure that it happened. The reasons women gave for supporting the child's contact included:

- despite the domestic violence, the partner was a 'good father'
- the children wanted to see the father
- women believed their children needed to know their father
- contact was seen as a way of ensuring fathers took some responsibility for their children, especially if the father had not been married or had denied the paternity of the child
- having left the father, some women did not want to be in the position of also preventing contact and having to cope with a child's subsequent anger
- preserving cultural or religious links with the father, his family and/or community.

Women wanted contact to be worthwhile, to be safe and 'quality contact' for the child:

I had sort of wanted them to have contact with him, but I wanted them to have good access, you know, like quality contact...but he was taking drugs and he was drunk all the time and he'd say things...he used to say to the kids, 'I'm going to cut your mother's throat' and you know, he was really warped. (Cara, in Hester and Radford 1996a, p.25)

Some women felt the children still had the right to see the father, even if the parenting relationship was difficult and the children had been disturbed by witnessing and living with the domestic violence. Alice, a woman interviewed for the child contact study, was in this position.

### Alice

Alice's husband had been violent from the start of their marriage. His violence included throwing things at her, pulling her hair, biting her, stabbing her with a fork, controlling her movements outside the house, isolating her from friends and keeping her short of money. He was not directly violent to the children, two daughters, although they were both very frightened of him and withdrawn. (The older child was receiving counselling to help her deal with the effects of witnessing domestic violence.) Alice tried to leave a few times and eventually moved with the children to a domestic violence shelter. She got a protection order from the court but her husband breached this by harassing her with constant phone calls, breaking windows and eventually trying to blow up her house. The husband was sent to prison for three weeks. On release he immediately continued the harassment. There were more short periods in prison following further breaches of the protection order. The husband meanwhile applied to the court to see the children, but his application was not granted following his abusive behaviour during a mediation session at the court. He re-applied a year later and an order was made for contact to take place in a contact centre. The husband verbally abused Alice at the contact centre, and followed her home on one occasion. Contact stopped when the father was also seen to be verbally abusive to one of his new girlfriend's children.

Alice continued to feel ambivalent about her ex-husband's motives in pursuing contact and about the conflicts she felt between her own interests and those of the children. She had a strong desire for her children to have a relationship with their father and to be loved by him, and the enduring hope that contact might still be possible in the future. Alice felt that the children, especially the youngest, had had some positive experiences of contact with their father, although she recognized that they had been much happier since the contact stopped:

> They are singing and dancing and you know they mess round and that. They fight now which they didn't do before. They do normal things now…and they are much, much happier. They are more confident as well… They have definitely changed. ('Alice')

Alice's experiences show clearly that contact is unlikely to be of value to a child when it is unsafe. Safety needs to be a priority when contact is considered in the context of domestic violence. Alice's conclusion that in the end the children were better off with no contact is supported by an Australian study that found that children with no contact with fathers, or who were not afraid of them, recovered more quickly from domestic violence (Mertin 1995).

For most of the children included in our research, contact was set up with their fathers fairly soon after separation, so there was little opportunity for children to have a period of recovery from the stress of having lived with the abuse. The AMICA study found that a sizeable minority of children (28%) were initially pleased to see their fathers. A smaller number (4%) were said to have been 'more settled' and 'happier in themselves as a result'. Twenty-three per cent of the mothers in the contact study and 58 per cent of parents in the AMICA study at first tried to set up contact for their children informally by negotiating with the father. Although the majority of parents who separate do arrange contact for children themselves through informal negotiations, contact informally arranged soon after separation in the context of domestic violence tended to be short lived, although in the AMICA study just over one in nine of the parents still had informal arrangements for contact after two years. Having tried unsuccessfully to set up informal contact, many mothers changed their minds about the value of contact for their children. We found no evidence that mothers were 'hostile' and opposing contact with fathers without reason. Mothers objected to the continued contact for a number of reasons relating to the ex-partner's behaviour and its impact on the children:

- Seventy-seven per cent of the mothers who were against contact felt the ex-partner was a bad role model. The abusive behaviour that led to the separation had not changed nor been challenged by the courts.
- Sixty-four per cent said the ex-partner lacked commitment to parenting.
- Forty-nine per cent feared that contact would be unsafe for the child.

- Fifty-eight per cent feared contact would be unsafe for themselves (38% feared for their lives).

- Forty-eight per cent said the child did not want contact (Radford et al. 1999).

Cases where contact in the long run 'worked' (that is, so neither child nor mother were abused) were limited. Only seven women in the contact study eventually set up non-abusive contact for their children. The majority of children in the AMICA survey, described by their mothers as being initially pleased to see their fathers, subsequently showed signs of great distress as a result of the contact becoming abusive. Nine of the children subsequently developed inappropriate sexual behaviour, 9 expressed a wish to die, 21 suffered from bed wetting and 36 from nightmares.

The possibility of reconciliation was a strong feature in the 'success' of the contact visits, the non-resident father (temporarily) curbing violence and showing remorse in an effort to effect a reconciliation and regain control. If the violence resumed after the 'reconciliation', this would clearly not be a successful outcome for a child. More women reported some brief periods where contact temporarily 'worked', but then violence would flare up again and the arrangements would break down. For most though, the possibility of ongoing abuse from the ex-partner was an ever present part of the picture.

## Child contact as a route to woman abuse

Ninety-four per cent of women in the contact study and 92 per cent in the AMICA study were abused after separation as a result of the child contact arrangements. Violent men are able to use their access to children to track down, find, harass and further abuse ex-partners. Violence was most likely to occur when mothers had to meet fathers face to face when ferrying children to and from contact visits, or if staying to supervise the father themselves. An Australian study of 42 women's experiences of child contact after separating from violent men similarly found the majority, all but one of the women (97.5%), were abused after separation, while 85.7 per cent of women who were resident parents described violence associated with the child contact (Kaye, Stubbs and Tolmie 2003).

Protection orders did not adequately deter violence. Just under half the mothers in the AMICA study had protection orders, but 70 per cent of these were breached. Thirty per cent of the orders were breached more than three times. Contact arrangements complicated matters and made orders even less effective. Because courts assumed the woman would be safe if a protection order was in place, some women were expected to put aside their own fears and play a key role in organizing the children's contact visits:

> They [the court] suggested that contact should be in his house so that the baby could get used to the surroundings of his home… Can you imagine sitting in the room with somebody who's battered you to a pulp and trying to be friendly because if you didn't you'd be so frightened of what he might do? But he saw that not so much as seeing the child, he thought it's seeing me… It was on one of these visits that he raped me. ('Audrey' – contact study)

Making contact safe also became the mother's responsibility because of the limited availability of safe contact services (see Chapter 8).

Some women are forced to move away from the abuser to find safety. But safe relocation is increasingly more difficult because violent men discover ex-partner's whereabouts by applying for contact or visitation orders from the courts. Ex-partners were able to locate and further abuse over a third of the women in the AMICA study as a result of applications made to the courts. Nine mothers who were found were living in refuges or shelters at the time. Many of the women in the contact study complained about fathers pumping the children for information on their whereabouts and movements:

> He'd sort of take the kids around. Kay was four and he'd like go to the areas he'd thought the refuges were in until he'd get to the street where Kay would know and she'd point out the place where it was, twice…and both times, I mean what he would do like is get me on the street and take me home… I must have gone back to the refuge four or five times. ('Alyson')

Women and children are sometimes killed by violent men who have used child contact as the route to further abuse.

In England in 1997, Georgina McCarthy and her son fled to a domestic violence shelter. Her husband, Paul Russell, immediately applied to the court to find the son. Georgina's solicitor persuaded the court not to reveal her new address. However, within six weeks, Georgina had to confront her husband in court to respond to his application for child contact.

All the professionals working with Georgina recognized that she was in danger and they did their best to protect her. Nobody gave Paul Russell her address, but the location of the court hearing and interim contact visits and the addresses of witnesses gave him enough information about the general area where she could be found.

The court finally refused to grant Paul Russell contact but he already knew too much. On 9 May 1998, the day after Georgina obtained her final divorce decree, Paul Russell entered her home and killed her in front of her son. Paul Russell then abducted the boy, handing him over to a hospital four days later. Paul Russell was sentenced to life imprisonment for killing Georgina McCarthy. The child was adopted.

(Adapted from speech by Hilary Saunders, National Children's Officer, Women's Aid Federation of England, 2001)

---

Fatality reviews in the US and the UK have shown a strong association between homicides of women and children, domestic violence, child visitation and custody disputes (Websdale, Sheeran and Johnson 1999). Following the murder of Georgina McCarthy, the Children Act Sub-Committee proposed measures to improve safety to prevent this happening again (Advisory Board on Family Law 2000/2001). A survey of refuge workers asking them about contact cases affecting families they knew found that nearly half the 178 respondents were aware of cases since April 2001 where a violent parent had used contact proceedings to track down the former partner (Saunders and Barron 2003).

Faced with the persistent violence from ex-partners, some mothers see leaving the children with the abuser as their only option for (relative) peace:

> I gave my husband custody of my children because he had hounded me into the ground and nearly killed me. ('Hilary')

'Lorna', a woman interviewed during the child contact study, also had to make this difficult choice.

## Lorna

Lorna married her partner when she was 17 and they had two children, a boy and a girl. Violence started early in the relationship, happened 'all day every day', and included regular sexual abuse and rape. The husband never hit her in the face, but would sometimes wound her with a knife or make her cut herself. Because of the abuse, Lorna took an overdose. After four years of marriage, when the children were aged two and four, Lorna got a divorce. The ex-husband then forced a reconciliation on her. Three months later, he was back to his old ways so Lorna fled with the children to a domestic violence shelter. He pursued her and managed to persuade her to return. She left him a second time, but his threats, violence and cajoling again led to her return. Whenever Lorna left home to move into a shelter, she had wanted the children to maintain contact with their father. She said he wanted to see them and that they wanted to see him. Lorna believed that her husband should see his children and that he would not harm them, but she was very afraid of what he would do to her. Lorna had to manage difficult and dangerous negotiations with her ex-husband on her own. On one occasion, she contacted a social worker to ask for help arranging contact because she was too frightened to take the children to meet their father. The social worker refused to become involved. Lorna's solicitor then suggested that perhaps a family member could help. Her ex-mother-in-law agreed to escort the children to and from meetings with their father. Once he had the children, the father used the visits to find out from the children where Lorna was staying, driving them around different areas until they recognized where they and their mother were living. He was able to find her again and again and force her to go back home with him. To escape from him, Lorna moved with the children to a shelter or refuge in another part of the country. There was no communication for a whole month. Lorna then had several phone calls from the children's grandmother, saying that the ex-husband was so depressed by not seeing the children, he was suicidal. Lorna finally agreed to the children visiting the grandmother for two weeks, enabling them at the same time to see their father. A week into the stay, the father disappeared with both children. Lorna had no idea where the children were. He kept them hidden away for a month. He then allowed Lorna to telephone the children and on one occasion to briefly visit them, under the supervision of her ex-mother-in-law. By the final interview, Lorna had stopped seeing the children altogether. She was clearly upset by this but felt that they had settled and it would be unfair to move them from their familiar surroundings to where she was now living at the other end of the country. As she explained:

> I think they are quite happy really, especially because they like living with their grandmother as well…she is probably the only stable thing that has happened in nearly a year, because they were in three refuges, then moved here, and seeing him do [to Lorna] what he does. To go back to her house and where they belong is normal. It's some normality to what they'd been used to before it all happened. ('Lorna')

Lorna had to sever her relationship with the children because she was too frightened to pursue contact. Her ex-husband had again found her and was still harassing her, ringing her at home and at work and threatening to kill her. Hoping to find safety, she had to cut all ties with her children and disappear.

Men who are violent to their partners are more likely to seek custody and less likely to pay child support than are non-abusive men (Liss and Stahly 1993). Disturbingly, as Lorna's experience shows, the father's persistence in pursuing contact has a greater impact on the outcome for children than their welfare or the quality of care provided by either parent.

## Contact and the abuse of children

Everything that happens to children living in families where there is domestic violence also happens after separation, and sometimes the incidents are worse. Table 6.1 sets out findings from the AMICA study on the abuse children experienced as a result of contact. In the NSPCC study (Hester and Pearson 1998), an examination of child abuse case records showed a clear overlap between domestic violence to the mother and the physical, sexual or emotional abuse of children by their fathers during contact. The NSPCC had to carry out 're-covery' work with the children as a result.

Mothers in our child contact study and AMICA study similarly reported child abuse and neglect by the father, and the children witnessing domestic violence during contact meetings. As Table 6.1 shows, the AMICA study found mothers reported that children were much more likely to be abused when the supervision of contact visits was withdrawn.

Protecting children from abuse, especially from sexual abuse during contact visits, was said to be particularly difficult. One of the Asian mothers we interviewed for the contact study, 'Meera', discovered two years after separation, that the father was sexually abusing the four and a half-year-old daughter:

> He'd had the children...my mum had collected them and the next morning my mum phoned to say that [daughter] had been extremely odd; she said, 'We don't know what's wrong with her.' She said, 'She came in, she sat in a corner, she curled up, she wouldn't eat.' She said, 'I wasn't sure whether she was going to have asthma.' So we talked to her, she just didn't say anything. Wasn't until I took the washing downstairs and happened to drop her underwear on the stairs, and there was blood in all her underwear...so we took her to the doctor, the doctor said he felt she had been sexually abused... [Daughter taken to the hospital and police involved. Daughter

found to be intact.] ...the police said they felt something had happened, but unfortunately they couldn't prove it. Because there was insufficient evidence they couldn't stand a child up in court of that age and ask her questions... ('Meera')

| Table 6.1: Abusive contact and children | | | |
|---|---|---|---|
| | 1<br>Informal<br>'agreed'<br>(n=128) | 2<br>Court<br>order<br>(n=148) | 3<br>Unsupervised<br>(n=45) |
| Quizzed child for information on parent | 54% | 53% | 80% |
| Shouted and swore at child | 26% | 26% | 40% |
| Looked after child while drunk/on drugs | 28% | 24% | 33% |
| Threatened or tried to abduct child | 33% | 19% | 22% |
| Did abduct child | 10% | 14% | 11% |
| Left child unsupervised for hours | 21% | 16% | 18% |
| Hit or slapped child hard | 13% | 14% | 22% |
| Exposed child to criminal activities | 12% | 9% | 9% |
| Threatened to hurt child | – (3) | 7% | 9% |
| Sexually abused child (touching) | 9% | 8% | 13% |
| Sexually abused child (penetration) | – (2) | – (3) | 7% |
| Locked child in a room | – | 5% | 9% |
| Punched or kicked child in the body | 4% | – (4) | 4% |
| Threatened to kill child | – (2) | – (3) | – |
| Threw a heavy object at child | – (0) | – (2) | |
| Intentionally burned child | – (1) | – | – |

Key:
Column 1 – % of children who were abused in informally arranged contact visits.
Column 2 – % abused during court ordered contact (supervised and unsupervised).
Column 3 – % abused when previously supervised contact became unsupervised.

Source: Radford *et al.* 1999, p.20. Reproduced with permission from Women's Aid Federation of England.

After this, contact stopped for a while. A year later, the child started to talk about what happened:

> ...she said that her and Daddy played special games and that she's Barbie girl and Daddy is Barbie boy, and that's all we've been told. ('Meera')

The child had totally changed following the experience:

> She's a totally different child, she's now, I mean at first she was messing on the floor, she was bed wetting, she was having nightmares. ('Meera')

The father was not prosecuted for the sexual assault. As he had not then re-applied for contact with the child, social services no longer regarded the child as being at risk of harm and they withdrew their support from the family. The father then applied to court and was granted contact with the child at a contact centre (a centre that was not able to offer one-to-one supervision). At the end of our research, he had asked for unsupervised staying contact visits. It is hard to see what lasting benefit a child might gain from having regular meetings with a father who sexually abuses her, especially if no attempt has been made to confront and curb his abusive behaviour. A child has to be safe before any sensible decision can be made about contact with an abusive parent. It is also important to carefully consider the purpose of setting up contact for the child, particularly if there has been alleged sexual abuse.

Contact visits can often mean that children have to cope alone with violent fathers' attempts to draw them into the abuse and undermining of their mothers. Pumping the children for information on the mothers' whereabouts and involving them in plans to kill the mother were common complaints made about fathers who had contact. As one of the children we interviewed in the contact study explained, she was terrified that she might divulge information regarding her mother's whereabouts:

> sometimes because my dad like threatened to kill her – I'd go over there to see him, he would be like, you've got to let me in the refuge... ('Annie', aged 13)

Children tried to minimize the harm or keep the peace by holding back information from the father or mother, mediating between the two and covering up or toning down the violence and threats of abuse. Children felt responsible for the protection of their mothers and often their siblings as well (see Chapter 5).

Many women reported problems with the children's health or behaviour which they attributed to the contact visits. The effects are similar to those shown by children when living with the father (see Chapters 4 and 5). They included bed wetting, incontinence during the day, incontinence when meeting the father, nightmares, agoraphobia, delayed speech or development, returning from contact and verbally or physically abusing the mother, stealing from her, playing pranks on her or following a father's orders to spy upon her. Women found it difficult to get the courts to accept that children's behavioural problems were due to difficulties with the contact rather than the result of separation from the father:

> I was in that awful position where I had been told by the social workers, I had been told by the solicitors if I didn't make her go every week that I would lose her… And so we spent an hour calming her down and we had to make her go on a visit after what had happened [father's assault on mother witnessed by child] … She came back and she just laid on the sofa all limp and just like curled up… I felt guilty beyond belief at making her go and it was this awful trap you are in, that you are told you have to make this child go and this child is looking at you for protection. ('Martha')

As shown in Chapters 4 and 5, children who have lived with domestic violence tend to have more adjustment difficulties than children from non-violent homes. There may be longer term detrimental impacts on children where contact is enforced despite parental conflict and opposition (Johnston 1993; Sturge and Glaser 2000).

## Taking children's views into account

Article 12 of the UN Convention on the Rights of the Child sets out the child's right to participate in decisions that affect their welfare:

> States Parties shall assure to the child who is capable of forming his or her own views the right to express those views freely in all matters affecting the child, the views of the child being given due weight in accordance with the age and maturity of the child.

> For this purpose, the child shall in particular be provided with the opportunity to be heard in any judicial and administrative proceedings affecting the child, either directly, or through a representative or an appropriate body, in a manner consistent with the procedural rules of national law.

Research shows that children want to be consulted about contact and residency but they do not expect to have to make the decisions for their parents (Hunt and Roberts 2004). In English and Welsh law, the welfare checklist in section 1 of the Children Act 1989 directs courts to take into account the ascertainable wishes and feelings of the child. Whether or not a child's wishes will be heard depends upon how receptive the parents are to their needs and the practice of professionals the child has contact with (Hunt and Roberts 2004). Neither mediators nor solicitors in the UK and the US tend to see children separately. Children may not be asked their views unless they see a CAFCASS (Children and Family Courts Advice and Support Service) practitioner in the UK or a custody evaluator in the US, or have separate advocacy or legal representation. In England and Wales, CAFCASS practitioners have less time to work directly with children because of a shift in practice from investigation to court reporting and also because of the long-standing under-resourcing in CAFCASS, the agency that works with children in the courts. In our contact research, we found only eight instances out of a total of 53 cases where court welfare officers (now called CAFCASS practitioners) had directly tried to ascertain children's views about contact with the absent parent (Hester and Radford 1996a).

Where professionals do talk with or observe children, there are great variations in the way this information is interpreted or the extent to which it is incorporated in decisions about contact. For instance, professionals may feel that the parents are best able to articulate the views of the children, and that what children say cannot be taken at face value. Children are not always listened to as separate individuals, and professionals' own value judgements and beliefs may take precedence.

It can take time to develop the trust with a child that is needed for a professional to ascertain the child's wishes. One refuge worker in our contact study had experienced this with some children in the refuge:

> when the welfare officer went to speak to them they wouldn't say anything, so access was granted…and then little by little it started coming out and eventually they stopped the access. (Refuge worker)

Even if a child does not have the verbal skills to express her/his wishes directly, there could be many non-verbal indications, which would only be picked up through close observation and investigation. For instance, in one example we were given, a four-year-old girl was seen by refuge or shelter workers to be adversely affected by contact with her father:

> she may not have been old enough to actually say what was going on, but she was old enough to, like show signs of real depression and withdrawal in a normally bright and bubbly child… (Refuge/shelter worker)

Many children, despite violence to their mothers or themselves, wish to see their fathers, but some children do not. It is often difficult for children to say that they do *not* want contact with their father. The dynamics of parent–child relationships are such that this might be a very difficult thing for children to do. Professionals may also dismiss or ignore children's views due to concerns that they may have been unduly influenced by their mothers. As a result, contact might be established even when children do not want it, or when it is not in the best interests of the child.

## Battery by the law

Many of the women who participated in the contact and the AMICA research studies were greatly stressed and disillusioned by the law. Some had repeatedly applied for protection orders that were not enforced. Many had been to court time and again to defend themselves and the children against a father's applications for changes to the contact arrangements. Although court procedures and the approach taken by CAFCASS policy in particular have changed recently, the family courts and wide 'unnacceptable' variations in practice (HMICA 2005) still give violent men ample opportunity for 'legal battery' by allowing expensive and exhausting investigations within the intimidating context of agreement seeking and mediation. Women and children end up being abused and impoverished by the court processes. Although her experience pre-dates policy changes introduced since the year 2000, Rachel's experiences illustrate this process of legalized secondary assault on women and children, where the seemingly ever open option go back to court, ignore the violence, delay procedures, and impoverish and intimidate an ex-partner persists:

*Rachel*

Rachel's husband initially assaulted her during her first pregnancy. He was then physically, mentally and emotionally abusive throughout the relationship. Rachel finally left the relationship when the police helped her move to a domestic violence refuge, leaving the children behind. She later applied to court to have the children join her. The father was granted contact twice a week. Nobody could be found to help with the contact visits so Rachel had to take the children herself to meet their father. She was regularly threatened and verbally abused, and on one occasion was physically attacked by him. The harassment continued via telephone and letter. Following an attempted assault at her new address after leaving the refuge, the ex-husband was sent to prison for two weeks for breaching a protection order. The case went back to court for contact to be re-arranged as the father had moved on his release and would not reveal his new address. His harassment of Rachel resumed and he started phoning the police saying that she was neglecting the children. The family had at this stage been to court eight or nine times to settle the contact arrangements. The judge ordered that taxis be used to ferry the children to and from contact, so that Rachel would no longer have to meet the father when visits were arranged. The harassment continued. Eventually, Rachel refused to co-operate with the contact meetings. Contact was next informally arranged with the help of a court welfare officer. This continued for a number of months until the younger son decided he no longer wanted to see his father. Rachel was impoverished because her ex-partner dragged her into repeated court hearings over the contact arrangements. While married, she and her husband owned their own house and Rachel had her own business. The cost of repeated court cases meant that Rachel lost her home and her business, moved into social housing and lived on state benefits.

The AMICA study similarly found that women separating from violent men became involved in a high number of court disputes over child contact. Nineteen per cent of the parents had been involved in seven to ten court cases, 13 per cent had been involved in more than ten cases. One mother had been involved in 30 cases. The social and economic costs of this litigation are so substantial that a sound argument could be made for diverting resources towards advocacy projects and safe contact services.

In the next chapter, we discuss in more detail battery by the law, and argue that it is possible because the law's response to domestic violence and contact for children is a victim-blaming response. The primary concern in the family courts is in getting women to overcome their fears for the sake of their children rather than challenging the violence of men.

## Conclusion

In this chapter, we have shown how important it is for professionals to be aware that violent men may use access to children to try to regain power and control over their ex-partners. The problem of domestic violence and child contact is broader than preventing direct physical or sexual abuse of the child and guarding against their witnessing domestic violence to their mothers. Contact is also used by violent men to undermine and harass the mother, to sustain her fears, with the subsequent detrimental impact upon her health, or to control her movements and activities after separation. Domestic violence perpetrators often try to draw children into the abuse and harassment of their mothers by:

- forcing them to join in the violence or harassment
- pumping them for information about the mother's movements and activities
- using children to track down mothers who have moved away
- getting the children, sometimes unwittingly, to relay threats
- influencing the children's beliefs or behaviour in order to undermine the mother's parenting.

As a result, mothers and children are at great risk of continued abuse after separation. Children are especially vulnerable to abuse and neglect and may find themselves with overwhelming responsibility to try to manage the father's behaviour and act as protectors for their mothers and siblings. Despite the risk of further violence to themselves, mothers may want children to have contact with their fathers after separation. In Chapter 7, we argue that more emphasis should be placed upon challenging the violence if children are to be safe.

# 7

# Mother Blaming in the Courts

In this chapter, we expand the argument about gender entrapment by showing how the law and court processes reinforce domestic violence perpetrators' efforts to regain power and control in contact cases. In family law, separated fathers are put into the position of the aggrieved, seen as deprived of their children. Although courts have started to take domestic violence into account when contact decisions are made, fear of hostile mothers alienating children from fathers has been the greater concern. This has reinforced violent men's tendency towards legal persistence and litigation abuse. The law's response to domestic violence and contact for children is a victim- and woman-blaming response. The primary concern in the family courts is in getting women to overcome their fears for the apparent sake of their children rather than challenging the violence of men. Courts may order supervised contact or attach conditions to an order to keep parents apart, but the purpose and value of contact for the child is rarely considered. Keeping in contact with fathers is almost always viewed as being in a child's best interests (Hester and Harne 1999; Mason 1999). We conclude this chapter by arguing that the value of setting up visits between a child and a violent man needs to be more thoroughly examined. More attention should be given to the needs, wishes and safety of children, the quality of the relationship with the violent parent and the well-being of the parent responsible for their everyday care.

## Responsible parenting and battery by the law

The following five key assumptions about 'responsible parenting' have been especially influential in the family courts in the UK and the US:

1. Most parents are 'reasonable parents' who can be encouraged to make decisions that are the best decisions for their children.

2.  It is best if parents can agree to decide things for themselves rather than bother the courts.

3.  Co-parenting, 'shared care' or generous contact are the top three outcomes for children when parents part.

4.  Mothers who do not facilitate shared care or generous contact are selfish and unreasonable and possibly child alienators.

5.  The best cure for maternal resistance is the enforcement of orders that support the father's contact with the child.

These assumptions have drawn upon a range of different arguments for reform of the family law from the mediation movement arguments about alternate dispute resolution, negotiation and child welfare (Haynes 1990) to the father's rights campaign for 'equal' parenting (Families Need Fathers 1993). Whatever the drivers, separated fathers are put into the position of the aggrieved, creating a cultural system of beliefs that are ripe for manipulation by abusers. In the rest of this chapter, we will explain how these assumptions about responsible parenting contribute to women's further abuse and victimization by the law.

We argued in Chapters 2, 4 and 6 that domestic violence perpetrators use a mixture of force, threat, fear and humiliation to bully and control partners. The left-hand column in Table 7.1 (perpetrator's abuse) summarizes our arguments in Chapter 6 about post-separation abuse and child contact. The right-hand column shows how, unfortunately, the law's response in the context of the five assumptions can reinforce rather than challenge the abusive behaviour of perpetrators.

### Keeping the secret of family violence

The first problem women encounter is that the domestic violence may not be considered because it is not identified as an issue relevant to the case. The legal process of arranging contact may not give a frightened person any opportunity to safely disclose her fears about the violence. Our national study of court welfare officers' practice found only a minority routinely asked or gave parents the opportunity to disclose experiences of domestic violence (Hester et al. 1997).

While mediators in the US and the UK have since introduced routine screening for domestic violence, up until recently there has been the widespread belief in the legal process that, if domestic violence is a concern, then it will inevitably 'come up' in the course of the proceedings (Hester et al. 1997). This assumes an ability and readiness among women living with domestic

**Table 7.1: How the family law reinforces
the behaviour of domestic violence perpetrators**

| Perpetrator's abuse | Battery by the law |
| --- | --- |
| Keeping the secret of family violence | Failure to screen – no routine enquiry<br>Courts rely on violence 'coming up' |
| Causing fear | Unsafe premises and court processes |
| Owning reality | Man's view dominates in joint meetings<br>His version of events is more believable |
| Manipulation and bullying | The emphasis on agreement results in coerced agreements |
| Victim blaming | Failure to explore 'hostility' to contact |
| Abuse of the children | Child's wishes and feelings inadequately considered |
| Abuse of the mother through abuse of the child | Failure to consider the purpose of contact |
| Child witnessing violence | Failure to address the safety of contact |
| Involving the wider family in the abuse | Allowing the family to supervise contact |
| Using children as ransom | Failure to consider the impact of violence on the child |
| Implicating children in the abuse | Failure to address the abuser's 'fitness' for contact |
| Harassment | Repeat applications to court |
| Undermining the mother's parenting | Failure to support the mother's capacity to care for the child |
| Breaking the emotional bond between mother and child | Forcing the mother to make the child comply with a contact order against his/her wishes |

violence to talk about the abuse, but this is not supported from findings from research. A range of complex reasons and feelings (fear, shame, love, duty) have been found to explain why women and children keep domestic violence secret (Glass 1995; Hoff 1990; McGee 2000). A recent inspection of

CAFCASS (Children's Family Courts Advisory and Support Service) practice found that, although it is suggested that 70 per cent or more cases involve domestic violence, there was still a failure to screen (HMICA 2005). Concerns about this failure to ask have resulted in the development of new domestic violence screening forms for all contact applications which were introduced in English family courts in 2005. Early observations by CAFCASS found the new forms indeed revealed a high number of cases involving domestic violence (Douglas 2005).

### Silenced by fear and coerced into agreement

The pressures put on mothers to negotiate and agree with partners can cause great fear for women who have experienced domestic violence (HMICA 2005), and may encourage them to consent to unworkable arrangements merely to get out of the frightening experience of having to see the abuser in court. The preference for parental agreement places parents who can agree in the position of being more 'reasonable' than parents who cannot. The presumption that parents will usually make agreements that are best or most workable for their children is fundamentally flawed in domestic violence cases, and results in coerced agreements that turn out to be unworkable (Hester and Radford 1996a). It is very unlikely that a woman will feel able to make a fair agreement about contact in the context of a relationship where the partner's controlling behaviour has involved manipulation, bullying and mind control where his perceptions of 'reality' have dominated (see the discussion in Chapter 3 of Madeleine's experiences of 'walking on eggshells').

Research suggests that men who are perpetrators of domestic violence are more likely to be granted contact with their children after separation than are men involved in cases where no violence is alleged (Liss and Stahly 1993). O'Sullivan looked at court files in the US and found that fathers who were subject to restraining or protection orders had a much higher rate of getting visits than men without these orders (O'Sullivan 2000).

Even where solicitors and other professionals have become aware of a history of domestic violence, this may be dismissed as being irrelevant to the well-being of the child, or simply ignored (HMICA 2005). It has been noted by other researchers that in some states in the US 'friendly parent provisions', where courts give preference in custody decisions to the parent most likely to give frequent contact, conflict with the requirement to take domestic violence into account (Jaffe *et al.* 2003). The abusive father can appear to be more 'friendly' (by wanting contact) than the mother (who fears it). Women are put in the difficult position of having to try to appear to the court to be 'friendly', unless the law specifically states that these provisions are irrelevant in domestic violence cases. In England, the AMICA (Aid for Mothers Involved in Contact Applications) study of 130 abused parents' experiences of contact cases involving 215 children found that high levels of violence to mothers and children during the relationships were not taken into account in court decisions about contact. Some mothers were advised by their lawyers not to mention it for fear they may not be perceived as being 'reasonable' (Radford *et al.* 1999).

There are also issues about the credibility of men's and women's claims in mediation and family court cases (Grillo 1991). Women who have experienced domestic violence are disadvantaged in mediation and court cases by the context of power inequalities. A fearful woman may be perceived as 'untogether' and unco-operative while her partner comes across as 'cool' and controlled. A fearful and possibly angry woman may not be the 'model' victim a judge expects to see. On the other hand, acting too calmly may also undermine a woman's credibility as a victim and tempt a judge to conclude that she can really cope with the abuse all by herself (Radford 2004b).

The point in time when women speak about domestic violence can affect their credibility. It may not be until after separation that a woman will have the confidence to talk about the harm caused to her children by living with the domestic violence. This leaves it open for the abuser to assert that the woman has another motive for raising these issues after separation, as she did not say anything before.

For many domestic violence cases, the evidence to support allegations may not be straightforward and is likely to be challenged in court. This is particularly so for sexual abuse as many women are reluctant to report the abuse to the police or to social services. Family courts in England (and in New Zealand) assess the evidence according to the civil law standard on the balance of probabilities, commensurate with the gravity of the allegation. The standard of evidence in family cases is less stringent than in a criminal case but it still presents difficulties for women and children who make allegations of abuse. In *Re H (Minors) (Sexual Abuse: Standard of Proof)* [1996] AC 563 in the English Court of Appeal, it was argued that the more serious the allegation of abuse, the greater the evidence required to accept it. Courts take a snapshot view of the evidence, assessing the credibility of each single alleged incident, rather than assessing the overall context of a pattern of behaviour. Further, lack of corroboration is a particular difficulty, especially when abuse is alleged to have happened to a very young child. Even if there is medical evidence of penetrative abuse to a child, a court could argue that lack of corroboration prevents them from linking this to the father/partner.

Abuse to one child is not necessarily seen as a threat to another. An example of this thinking is illustrated in H v G [2003] NZFLR 985, a case in the New Zealand family courts, where it was accepted that the child had been sexually abused but there was no corroborative evidence to support the mother's allegation that the father was responsible. The father was given unsupervised contact because the judge believed that there was no real threat to the child. The mother's heightened fears of sexual abuse became part of the problem because they were viewed by the judge to result from the mother's own past experiences of abuse as a child. Previous victimization, as in this case, can be seen to make women over-sensitive to the risk of abuse. This conclusion then can lead a court to recommend that the main solution to contact difficulties will be therapy for the mother (see later for further discussion).

### Failure to consider the purpose of contact because shared care is the norm

The emphasis upon unquestioned parental agreement as the best option means that there is no assessment of the purpose and value of contact for the individual child. This also works to exclude children from consultation about agreements that are made (see HMICA 2005). We argued in Chapter 6 that children's views about contact are not considered adequately and this can result in further abuse of the children when they have unsafe and unwanted contact.

Fathers' rights groups in many countries have supported the development of joint custody, 'co-parenting' and shared care of children on separation and divorce. In the US, joint custody was introduced in 1980 in California. It is now an option for the courts in nearly all states, the preferred option in some and in others it has been imposed on parents against their wills (Mason 1999). Courts have assumed that, if both parents are awarded joint custody, this will lead to more equitable, 'gender neutral' arrangements being made about the care of the children. This trend has been a dangerous one for women and children living with domestic violence because it has created an expectation that a 'good mother' will, after separation, support the father having plentiful contact with the children. Joint custody has caused huge problems for women and children living with domestic violence because of the difficulties in sharing decision making about children, or jointly managing their care. It appears that the courts used joint custody more to appease parents in conflict than to meet the needs of children (Mason 1999). A study of the custody decisions for 908 families in California found that joint physical custody (where the parents are awarded joint physical care of the child) was the outcome for nearly one-fifth of the families. A large number of these had a history of 'intense' parental conflict. Nearly all had been negotiated through a mediator or an attorney, rather than decided in the courts (California at the time had mandatory mediation). Fathers tended to apply for joint physical custody and cut their child support payments on the basis that they were also caring for the children. However, over the two-year period of the study, joint physical custody for many of the children saw some 'mother drift'. Despite having the order for joint physical custody, children continued to spend most of their time with their mothers. Fewer than half the children who had joint physical custody in an American study spent more than three to four nights in a two-week period with their fathers (Maccoby and Mnookin 1992).

Joint custody, whether physical or purely legal, gives the abusive partner a free rein to use the children to get access to the mother. A number of states in the US, including California, now require courts to consider domestic violence as a presumption against joint custody or prohibit joint custody being awarded when it has been found that domestic violence has occurred (Lemon 1996).

There have been similar trends, spurred on by concerns about equal parenting and 'father deprivation', in many European countries and in Australia, Canada and New Zealand (Jaffe *et al.* 2003). In some countries, including Denmark and Poland, the idea that mothers and fathers should (be able to) parent jointly and preferably without interference from the state, has led to difficulties for women. In Poland, what Fuszara (1997) calls 'joint parental rights' means that both parents have to participate in all official decisions concerning the child 'regardless of whether the second parent has any contact with the child whatsoever and whether the child's fate concerns him'. This allows an abusive parent with no interest in a child to have a stake in decisions. In Denmark, the notion of 'joint parental authority' has likewise created difficulties (Hester 2005). For instance, in cases where a child has been kidnapped or not returned by the father after a visit, the authorities have been loath to intervene as both parents are seen to have equal authority (Hester and Radford 1996a). It is hard to see how this benefits children. In Denmark, the emphasis on joint parenting has led to increasing numbers of child abuse cases being reported to children's organizations (Hester 2002, 2005).

*Safety is ignored because the benefits of maintaining contact outweigh possible harm*

The AMICA research found the majority of parents were abused when contact was set up and the children were said to have suffered emotional abuse from the exposure to ongoing violence and harassment. Ninety-two per cent of the parents and 76 per cent of the children were subsequently said to have been abused on contact (physically, sexually or psychologically). Seventy per cent of the children who said they did not want contact with the father had contact ordered by courts. Only 35 per cent of the children had welfare reports ordered. Twenty per cent of the children subject to welfare reports were not seen by a court welfare officer. These findings suggest poor levels of consultation with children, reinforced by research by O'Quigley (2000), which found work with children in the family courts in England ranged widely from very good to non-existent, and by a recent inspection of CAFCASS and the family courts by HMICA (2005). Children are put at risk because of the failure to consider the possibility of manipulation by the violent parent during contact visits.

Although many courts are now required by law to take domestic violence into account, women still find that the violence they have experienced is disregarded as irrelevant to the welfare of their children. It can be difficult to persuade a judge to accept that the harm or potential harm of exposure to domestic violence is a greater risk to a child than not seeing the father. In England, 'cogent reasons' have to be found before courts consider stopping contact. Evidence of harm to the child would usually be a cogent reason. But harm can be dismissed as a 'transient problem'. In the case of *Re O* [1995] 2 FLR 124, the judge argued:

> The courts should not at all readily accept that the child's welfare will be injured by direct contact. Judging that question the court should take a medium-term and long-term view of the child's development and not accord excessive weight to what appear likely to be short-term or transient problems.

Reasons for denying contact were considered in light of the long-term harm which may result from the child losing the father. Courts are urged to consider:

> [whether] the fundamental emotional need of every child to have an enduring relationship with both his parent…(is) outweighed by the depth of harm which, in light, inter alia, of his wishes and feelings…this child would be at risk of suffering…by virtue of a contact order. (*Re M* [1995] 1 FLR 274)

It would be difficult to argue against stopping contact given this logic, because the benefits of having contact with the father (if any) might only become apparent in the long term.

*Re P* [1996] 2 FLR 314 is an example of a case in the English courts where the unsuitability of the father was overlooked and the mother's objections disregarded. In this case, the father had tried to strangle the mother and made attempts to kill the children. He was sentenced to prison for 12 months. On release, he had 'supervised' meetings with the children at a contact centre, but this stopped following the mother's application. Psychiatric evidence was presented in support of the mother's objections. This showed the meetings were causing distress to one of the children, and that the child did not want them to continue. The mother argued that anxiety about the meetings and fear of the father's violence were undermining her health and ability to care for the children. There was also evidence that the father held Nazi sympathies, including a photograph he had taken of the children dressed up in Nazi regalia. Looking at the mother's medical evidence, the judge in the case argued that the court should consider:

> Does [the] evidence...support the proposition that the possible detriment to the children of not seeing their father is outweighed by the possible detriment to them through a threat to their mother's health caused by stress or anxiety? (*Re P* [1996] 2 FLR 314)

Describing the father's conduct as 'exemplary', the mother's case was dismissed and it was asserted that she 'should be able to cope'. The court upheld the father's appeal on the grounds that too much weight had been placed on the risk of emotional harm to the children arising from the mother's anxiety and deteriorating health. *Re P* [1996] 2 FLR 314 demonstrates how courts are able to displace men's responsibilities for domestic violence by constructing women's fears as unreasonable, disproportionate and harmful to their children.

Time is another obstacle women face in getting courts to take domestic violence seriously. Judges expect women to overcome their fears in a short period of time. The time allowed bears no relation to any research findings on overcoming abuse or on the time needed to reform a perpetrator. A stepped approach to contact may be set up to get women to 'move on'. This means that contact in the context of domestic violence is approached in a similar way to phobia therapy, where it is assumed that gradual, increasing exposure to the source of fear will eliminate it altogether. Contact is set up so that it starts off with a gradual re-introduction of the father (through 'indirect contact' via letters, photos or phone calls) and then progresses through stages from supervision towards the 'ideal' of unsupervised overnight stays and shared care. This rigid approach creates particular difficulties for women who have suffered sexual and emotional abuse where the main evidence of harm result-ing from the abuse is likely to be the distress of the victim, and where the distress can take some years to overcome. The approach appeals to liberal beliefs in change for the better and rehabilitation, but requires no effort on the practitioner's part to do anything to bring this about by dealing with the primary cause of the problem, i.e. the behaviour of the perpetrator. The approach is based on the assumption that, no matter what the previous pattern of behaviour, most fathers can eventually be relied upon to offer some benefit to their children. Courts' reluctance to stop contact leaves women and children living often for years with the threat and fear of ongoing abuse. In the longer term, this poses a risk to the well-being of the mother, and to the child's emotional security as a result of not having peace at home.

### Failure to consider the abuser's 'fitness' for contact

A perverse finding from the child contact research was that professionals working with the family courts put more effort into getting mothers to overcome their fears and co-operate than on ensuring women and children at risk of abuse would be safe (Hester and Radford 1996a). Very little attention was given to addressing fathers' responsibilities to stop the violence. The law in England has lagged behind the US, Australia and New Zealand in this respect, and only recently have we seen any proposals to enable family courts to order attendance on perpetrator or parenting programmes (DCA 2004). Violent men often blame their partners for the violence happening. Courts are less likely to do this, but the victim-blaming outcome is similar and results from the overwhelming focus on the victim's fears rather than on the perpetra-tor's behaviour as a primary block to child contact. Failure to consider whether or not a violent parent has any capacity to stop the violence puts children at risk of the emotional harm of being drawn into further abuse of the mother.

In England, a married or previously married violent father has parental responsibility for his child, regardless of his 'fitness' or ability to provide any parenting care. Unmarried fathers can apply for parental responsibility and are seldom refused, even if they are violent. The number of contact applica-tions refused by courts is still declining. This has increased violent men's scope to stay involved in their ex-partners' lives. Although it looks like joint custody called something else, having parental responsibility is not supposed to mean that fathers have the 'right to interfere in the day to day management of a child's life' (*Wall J Re P (A Minor) (Parental Responsibility Order)* [1994] 1 FLR 578). Fathers who do not live with their children have responsibilities and rights but may not be able to exercise these in practice unless they have contact with the children. The parent currently looking after the child makes the day-to-day decisions. This means that if, for instance, a child should fall ill on a holiday with the father, the father would be able to give consent for medical treatment. If a dispute should arise over the child's upbringing or care, e.g. over the child's name, education or medical care, parents are able to go back to court to ask for a solution (a 'specific issues' order). In principle, this allows arrangements to be made more for the benefit of children than under the joint custody provisions in American law. There is, however, much confusion among people working with children about what parental responsibility involves. Violent men have exploited this uncertainty and have been able to track down their ex-partners by obtaining information from schools or nurseries (Hester and Radford 1996a; Radford *et al.* 1999). This has made it more difficult for women fleeing abusive partners to move away and remain safe.

### Repeat applications to court

In Chapter 6 we discussed how women and children can be impoverished and exhausted by an ex-partner's repeat applications for contact from the family courts. It can be very difficult to prevent litigation abuse, and cases that are stopped for being 'vexatious' tend to have persisted to the extreme. One example was a case in England concerning a father's rights campaigner called Mr Harris, who had logged over 120 court appearances in his protracted contact dispute before the court put a stop on any further applications (Radford 2004b).

### False allegations and unreasonable fears

A recent report on CAFCASS and the family courts found CAFCASS practitioners when writing reports too often adopt a 'narrative approach' which describes what each party in a case says without giving sufficient analysis or making any attempt to use what was said for assessment. This leads to a 'he said/she said' context (HMICA 2005) that strongly disadvantages women who have lived with violent partners. The context of disbelief over allegations of domestic violence and sexual abuse in the courts urgently needs to be changed if women and children are to be safe. In this section, we look critically at claims that women frequently make false allegations about abuse to prevent fathers having contact with children, and we argue that assessments should draw upon evidence from research.

Elizabeth Morgan's efforts to prevent contact visits between her ex-husband and her daughter Ellen was perhaps the most notorious and lengthy case in recent years (Mason 1999). The veracity of the mother's allegations about abuse was widely contested. Elizabeth Morgan alleged her ex-husband had sexually abused her daughter Ellen on contact visits since she was two years old. The case attracted extensive publicity in the 1980s and 1990s. Elizabeth Morgan, a plastic surgeon, removed her daughter to a secret address and then overseas to prevent court-ordered visitation from happening. She was imprisoned for contempt of court for disobeying the visitation order. Elizabeth Morgan said she was trying to protect her child but her ex-partner claimed she had made false allegations of sexual abuse and had fabricated the evidence to break his relationship with his daughter. He argued that Elizabeth had coached her young daughter and had even staged and video-taped her re-enactment of the abuse. Ellen, liable also to be seen as in contempt of court, remained exiled in New Zealand until a special bill was passed in Columbia in 1996 temporarily allowing children aged 13 or over to choose whether or not to visit a non-custodial parent. Elizabeth Morgan gave up her job, went to prison and sent her child thousands of miles overseas. That a mother and child would go to these lengths to get around an order for visitation without good reason beggars belief. Yet, there exists a pervasive fear that mothers will make false allegations and fabricate evidence about violence or sexual abuse in order to claim 'ownership' of children and to stop fathers having any contact with them.

These concerns surface time and again in court discussions of 'parental alienation syndrome' (PAS), 'maternal hostility' and the 'obstructive' or 'sabotaging' mother, and, more recently, in concerns that supposedly mentally ill women suffer from delusions about threats to the safety of children. In America, Richard Gardner, clinical professor of child psychiatry at Columbia University, first coined the term 'parental alienation syndrome' to explain why (he believed) there were so many false allegations of child sexual abuse in the courts. According to Gardner, PAS describes a situation that results from behaviour of one parent (usually the resident parent and nearly always the mother) that is designed to denigrate and create hostility in the child against the other parent (usually the non-resident parent who is nearly always the father). PAS results when the alienating behaviour of the parent combines with the child's own contribution to the disparagement of the parent (Gardner 1985). The purpose of PAS is to align the child with one parent (usually the mother) so that the other parent (usually the father) is forced out of the child's life. Children affected by parental alienation syndrome exhibit a cluster of up to eight behavioural symptoms (see www.rgardner.com for details). Basically, the child is seen as 'programmed' by the mother into rejecting and fearing the other parent, viewing them as 'bad' or harmful, and wanting them out of their lives. It is argued that the longer PAS is allowed to continue the harder it is to overcome and the more detrimental to the welfare of the child.

Gardner has said that PAS is not a relevant concept to be applied if abuse is real (Gould 1998) and he developed criteria which he argued would help professionals to distinguish between credible and false allegations (see www.rgardner.com). According to Gardner, testimony on PAS was accepted in 67 court cases in the US, Canada, Australia and Germany since 1987, even though there is no sound empirical research to support the existence of this syndrome (see www.rgardner.com for Gardner's list of references to court cases, academic and practitioner publications). PAS has crept into British and European courts, despite the leading court ruling in England that accepted no evidence exists to support its existence (*Re L, V, M & H (Contact: Domestic Violence)* [2000] 2 FLR 334). PAS has been a scoop for fathers' rights groups and for abusers. Although Gardner publicly rejects any association with fathers' rights groups, PAS has been strategically employed by fathers' rights advocates in the US and Europe to get women's and children's compliance with access orders. Expert testimony has been used to discount children's claims that they fear their fathers. Children who refuse contact with their fathers are portrayed as victims not of abuse but of their mother's 'parental alienation'. The solution to PAS is to force the child to confront and thereby 'overcome' his/her fears by meeting with the father. Those who promote the idea of PAS believe, that if the child regularly has face-to-face contact with the father, then, over time, the paternal alienation and associated symptoms of distress will wane. 'Threat therapy' is used to ensure this happens. The 'therapy' consists of bullying and threatening children 'for their own good', threatening the child and mother with sanctions if visits do not go ahead. The sanctions are usually putting the mother in prison or transferring the child's residence to the father, but again there is little empirical evidence to confirm the efficacy of threat therapy for curbing alienation and meeting the needs of children (Gould 1998; Jaffe *et al.* 2003).

In the English courts, women's fears of abuse have similarly been dismissed on the grounds that the mothers are deluded, mentally ill or suffering from Munchausen Syndrome by Proxy. In Munchausen by Proxy, the sufferer harms a child to satisfy her own needs for attention. The best known case of this condition in England concerned the nurse Beverly Allitt, charged in 1991 for killing four children in the hospital ward where she worked. Munchausen

Syndrome by Proxy has been supported in family and criminal cases by testimony given by psychiatrists such as Professor Roy Meadows. The evidence base has been subject to criticism and Meadows' testimony in homicide cases was discounted on appeal. There is some worrying evidence from research in England that the syndrome has been used by violent fathers to victim blame and coerce their ex-partners. The AMICA study found 18 out of the 130 parents said that their fears of domestic violence were renamed Munchausen Syndrome by Proxy during court proceedings. A psychological assessment of the mother was carried out in 14 of these cases, and in eight cases where the results were known no evidence of the syndrome was found (Radford *et al.* 1999). A father's allegation that the mother may be suffering from Munchausen Syndrome by Proxy may be more credible to professionals working in the courts than his claim that she simply lied. It can be difficult for women to rebuke any allegation that she is responsible for the child's distress because supporting evidence of the father's abuse and harm to the child through exposure to domestic violence may be poor (more on this later).

At the root of these debates about PAS and maternal hostility rests the belief that courts are plagued by false allegations of domestic violence and abuse. There is no evidence to substantiate concerns that women frequently make false allegations to gain an 'advantage' in a contact case. A study of over 9000 divorce cases in the US found less than 2 per cent involved false allegations of abuse (Thoennes and Tjaden 1991). One reviewer of studies of false allegations concluded that false denials of abuse by perpetrators were much more commonly made than false allegations (Conte 1992). It seems that women are more likely to *under-report* domestic violence than they are to exaggerate. Two out of three women who experience violence from a partner do not disclose the abuse to an agency (Dominy and Radford 1996).

## Forcing women and children to comply

Women and children who do not comply with orders of the court are in contempt and liable to imprisonment. In 1996, Dawn Austin was sent to Holloway Prison in London for refusing to allow contact between her four-year-old daughter and her violent ex-partner. The ex-partner had served a prison sentence for breaking the jaw of his former wife, and had a history of serious violence against Dawn which the court accepted, but chose to disregard. Her objections to the father's contact were dismissed as 'flimsy', and her desire to protect her child as 'unwise' and 'misguided'. The appeal court over-ruled the paramount principle of the child's welfare by agreeing that the mother in this case should be sent to prison (*A v N (Committal: Refusal of Contact)* [1997] 1 FLR 533). Dawn's children were placed in care and a social worker arranged for contact to go ahead in her absence.

The actual imprisonment of women for contempt of court in contact cases in England is presently infrequent. The threat of imprisonment may be much more common and just as effective in bullying women into compliance with court orders which they see as harmful to their children. The AMICA study found 61 per cent of the mothers were threatened in some way, 39 per cent threatened with imprisonment but only two women were actually sent to prison (Radford *et al.* 1999). In America, more mothers and children have been incarcerated. In Illinois in 1995, 12-year-old Heidi Nussbaum was shackled in leg irons and ordered to a juvenile detention centre for refusing to visit her father. Her eight-year-old sister, Rachel, was 'grounded' by the judge and her mother expected to enforce the grounding. The judged dismissed as 'nonsense' the court-appointed psychologist's view that it was not in the children's interests to be forced to visit the father (Mason 1999). Similar cases are described by Murray (1999), including one case involving a seven-year-old boy who, despite throwing temper tantrums, crying hysterically and becoming physically abusive when faced with seeing the father, was placed in the Morris County Youth Shelter for the weekend for refusing visitation.

There has never been a case where a father has been imprisoned for not visiting his children. This legalized bullying of abused women and children exposes the victim-blaming logic on which the family courts' approach to child contact has been based. The courts are preoccupied with the mother's fears, her behaviour and her responsibility to make contact work. The man's responsibilities for causing these fears and any effort he may take at all to change or to offer his children a worthwhile relationship have been ignored although, as we show later, there are signs of some change. The reasons behind women's and children's opposition to contact need to be more sensitively investigated. It should not be assumed that a child's opposition to visits with the non-resident father will result from 'parental alienation'.

## Conclusion

In February 1994, three children from Wanganui in New Zealand – Tiffany, Holly and Claudia Bristol – were killed by the father who had been given interim custody of them three months earlier. The custody order was granted to the father at an ex-parte hearing, despite the fact that there had been a history of domestic violence from the father to the mother and there was currently an application for (another) protection order before the court. After the murder of the children, Christine Bristol called for a ministerial inquiry into the actions of the Family Court in awarding custody of the children to her violent husband. The inquiry recommended reforming the Guardianship Law so that domestic violence would be taken into account when decisions about child custody were made (Busch 1998). In 1995, the New Zealand Guardianship Amendment Act introduced a rebuttable presumption against unsupervised visitation where there has been domestic violence. Section 16B(4) of the Act states that the Family Court *shall not* make any order giving custody or unsupervised visitation to a party who has used violence against a child of the family or against the other party to the proceedings *unless* the Court is satisfied that the child will be safe while the violent party has custody of or access to the child. Section 16B(5) provides a list of statutory criteria to be considered by the courts when making decisions about safety. These include an assessment of the nature and seriousness of the violence, how recently and frequently it occurred, the likelihood of further violence, the physical or emotional harm caused to the child by the violence, and the opinions of the other party and the child regards safety (Busch 1998). The New Zealand law thus requires courts to make a detailed risk assessment in custody and access cases where there are allegations of domestic violence. An evaluation of the New Zealand Guardianship law found that the reforms had led to safer access arrangements for children and parents in the majority of cases reviewed, although some children were still being exposed to violence and emotional abuse (Chetwin *et al.* 1999; see also Radford 2004b).

Similar amendments to the law have been made in the US, Ireland and Australia, and they have been recently recommended in Canada and England and Wales (Bala *et al.* 1998; Children Act Sub-Committee 2000). Over 40 states in the US have included domestic violence among the 'best interest' factors to be evaluated by courts making custody and access decisions (Doyne *et al.* 1999; National Council of Juvenile and Family Court Judges 1994). The Model Code on Domestic and Family Violence of the National Council of Juvenile and Family Court Judges contains a rebuttable presumption that it is in the best interests of the child to reside with the non-abusing parent in a locality of the parent's choice. Some states, such as Louisianna, require the perpetrator of domestic violence to have successfully completed a treatment programme and not to be abusing alcohol or drugs before custody can be considered. Section 405 of the Model Code urges courts to consider granting visitation only if adequate provision can be made to ensure the safety of the child and the non-abusing parent. Hawaii now prohibits the perpetrator from having visitation unless adequate provision is made for the physical safety and *psychological well-being* of the child and for the physical safety of the victimized parent (National Council of Juvenile and Family Court Judges 1994). By 2000, 17 states had adopted the Model Code provisions on custody and ten included provisions on supervised visitation. Other amendments in the past few years include restricting access to weapons and firearms for domestic violence perpetrators, powers to prevent any visitation between children and a parent who has murdered the other parent, provisions for confidentiality and safe relocation and the introduction of *The Greenbook Initiative* in 1999 to model and monitor practice and safety issues in courts and communities (Schecter and Edleson 1999; for further information, see www.thegreenbook .info).

In the 1990s, the law was amended in Australia. The Family Law Reform Act 1995 (S68F and S68K) makes specific reference to domestic violence as a factor which courts should address when considering the welfare of children. Cases in the Australian courts established that, although the welfare of a child is usually served by having continuity of contact with the non-resident parent, the child may have a more compelling need for peace and tranquillity in the residential parent's home (*Sedgely v. Sedgely* [1995] FLC 92 623; *Irvine v. Irvine* [1995] FLC 92 624; *Grant and Grant* [1995] FLC 92 506). A series of court decisions established that there should be no contact where there is 'unacceptable risk' to the child. Unacceptable risk of harm to a child may be found to exist even when the child is not in danger of being physically abused or has not witnessed violence. The capacity of a violent and abusive man to parent effectively and provide an adequate role model for his children has also been doubted (*Patsalou and Patsalou* [1995] FLC 92 580).

In Northern Ireland in April 1998, the law changed so that, where protection (non-molestation) orders have been granted and contact or residence is applied for, courts effectively require a risk assessment by considering any possible harm to children from seeing or hearing domestic violence. In England and Wales, however, a review of the law rejected suggestions for reform based on the New Zealand approach (Children Act Sub-Committee 2000). In England and Wales and in Australia, the concern with 'father deprivation' has held much more sway upon the courts than any concern with risk or safety. Good practice guidelines were introduced in 2000 to assist the courts instead. The guidelines recommend courts make a finding of fact where domestic violence is alleged. If the domestic violence is accepted, the court then considers whether this is likely to affect the child's contact with the non-resident parent, paying particular attention to:

- any harm the child has suffered or is likely to suffer
- the non-resident parent's motivation in seeking contact
- his likely behaviour if granted contact
- and his capacity to change and to behave appropriately.

The guidelines also consider how to approach interim contact, ordering a welfare report and supervised contact. There are some similarities with the New Zealand approach, but judges in England have a great deal of discretion to determine for themselves the relative importance of domestic violence to contact cases. The effect of this can be seen directly in the Court of Appeal case in June 2000 where the guidelines were accepted but the judges warned against the 'pendulum swinging too far' to create an 'excessive concentration on past history and an over reflection on physical abuse' (*Re L, V, M & H (Contact: Domestic Violence)* [2000] 2 FLR 334). In the English courts, as in many states in the US, domestic violence remains one factor among others to be taken into account when considering the welfare of a child. A review of cases known to refuge workers in England for the Women's Aid Federation found 48 per cent said that unsafe contact orders were still being routinely made (Saunders 2001). Similarly, the recent review of family courts and CAFCASS practitioner responses found no formal risk assessment was made in any of the 56 CAFCASS interviews with families affected by domestic violence. The perception that there should be a contact presumption and the pressures exerted on parents to reach an agreement took priority so that the treatment of domestic violence cases was no different to cases where no violence was involved (HMICA 2005). There has not been a similar review or audit of the judicial approach to child contact cases in the context of domestic violence since this change in policy in 2000.

The Australian law similarly gives judges broad discretion over the relevance of domestic violence to a child's 'right' to contact. Tensions have developed between the right to contact principle set out in the Family Law Reform Act 1995 s60B(2) and the requirement not to expose a person to 'an unacceptable risk of family violence', set out in s68K. Solicitors and the courts have given precedence to the contact principle over domestic violence issues and, as a result, it has become more difficult for women fearful of further abuse to relocate or to obtain orders refusing contact. Prior to the Reform Act, access/contact was often suspended until trial because the allegations of violence had not been tested. Since the Act, the opposite has been the case: interim contact is set up until the domestic violence allegations are proved (Rhodes, Graycar and Harrison 1999). The Australian experience demonstrates the difficulties that result when legislation contains mixed messages about contact, abuse and the welfare of children. If domestic violence is accepted by the court, safety should be the primary consideration and not merely one factor among others.

Tensions persist, however, between the pro-contact drive towards enforcement and the efforts to make contact safe. Jaffe *et al.* (2003) argue convincingly that a totally different approach is needed in family court cases where there are allegations of violence and abuse. We will consider the issues for assessment in Chapter 8.

# 8

# Improving Safety for Women and Children after Separation

This chapter focuses on the practice issues raised by our previous discussion of post-separation violence and child contact. Women fearing domestic violence may nonetheless want their children to maintain contact with their fathers. Children may also express a wish to see their fathers. Who decides whether this will be safe? What is safety in this context? Child contact in the context of domestic violence is not just a matter of providing a safe venue for parents and children to meet. It can also involve undoing the harm caused to children (McMahon, Neville-Sorvilles and Schubert 1999) and possibly repairing or building an appropriate relationship between parent and child. Current thinking about contact needs to change radically to respond to the needs of children as individuals, so that safety, including the child's emotional safety and need for peace at home, takes precedence over the political commitment to keep fathers in touch with children.

## The need for assessment

In the last chapter, we argued that it is important to look at the purpose and value of contact between a child and a violent parent. This means that some-times it is necessary to consider whether there should be any contact at all. The family courts look bleakly on any delay in children's cases, but children who have lived with violence and abuse may need time to recover and cases where there are abuse allegations will take longer to assess. The type of contact that may be appropriate needs to match the *specific needs* of the child. The complexity of the different issues raised in cases involving violence and abuse can be illustrated in the following case studies:

## Can a violent man be a caring parent? What is the nature of the attachment between a child and a violent father?

Kelly (nine) and May (seven) are currently living in a women's refuge with their mother. Their mother left their father because of his escalating violence, culminating in a brutal attack with a broken bottle which left her in fear of her life. Despite her injuries, the mother has described the father as 'devoted' to the children and is concerned that they are missing him.

## In what circumstances will the stability and emotional safety of the child's current family be more important than supporting a relationship between the child and the biological father?

Martin is four years old. His mother separated from his father because of the domestic violence when Martin was just over a year old. Martin's mother moved 200 miles to get away from the violence and has now settled in a new relationship and recently married her new partner. Martin has a good relationship with his stepfather and no memory of his biological father. Martin's father has applied for visiting contact.

## To what extent do courts consider a child's emotional safety in the context of current family relationships, including relationships with siblings?

Jo (four) and Bea (three) live with their mother, her new partner and two (half) brothers, John (eight) and Michael (ten). John and Michael witnessed their stepfather's domestic violence to their mother and are very frightened of him. Jo and Bea remember their father even though they last saw him over a year ago. They are said to have no memory of the domestic violence. The father and his parents have applied for visiting contact.

## Can a child gain any benefit from having contact with the man who killed her mother?

Sukina is 12 years old and living with her grandparents. She last saw her father two years ago when he stabbed and killed her mother with a ten-inch kitchen knife. Sukina witnessed the murder and called the police and emergency services for help. Her father is now in prison and has asked her to visit him.

> **Are children adequately protected by the family courts when mothers raise concerns about child sexual abuse? Are the allegations investigated appropriately?**
>
> Charmaine is four years old and lives with her brother Richard (eight) and her mother. Both Richard and his mother had been sexually and physically abused by Charmaine's father although there was no prosecution. He has applied for contact with Charmaine.

The purpose of contact for the children concerned may be different in each of these cases and this affects the assessment issues (see Chapter 6 for a discussion of the different purposes contact may have). It is difficult to generalize about the circumstances and reasons in which contact might be wanted by, and worthwhile for, an individual child. The research discussed in this book would steer us clearly in the direction of caution faced with a request for regular face-to-face visiting contact, especially from a murderer, but it is still possible to imagine circumstances in all the case studies where *some* contact with the violent father at *some* point might be a worthwhile and positive experience for a child expressing a wish to have this. Indeed, this is why some jurisdictions have opted for rebuttable presumptions against contact in cases of violence and abuse.

Research by the child psychiatrists Harris Hendricks, Black and Kaplan (1993) is relevant to Sukina's case study. Harris Hendricks *et al.* looked into the experiences of 95 children whose fathers had killed their mothers. Despite their terrible and traumatizing experiences, some of the children wanted to visit their fathers, even if this was only one visit to tell him how they felt. Children who had witnessed substantial violence to the mother before her death were more likely to express the wish to preserve contact, possibly because they had learned a compulsion to care for the parent as a result of living with the abuse. None were in the position, however, of having to go for unsafe visiting contact soon after separation from the violent parent. The children who chose to visit their fathers had been prepared for this and they had been consulted. Good assessments are needed to ensure that any contact that is set up will be worthwhile and worth sustaining.

## Who decides?

In most of the earlier case studies, the children would be seen by the courts as too young to be able to express their wishes and feelings competently. Perhaps the most taxing cases before the courts involve children who are very young, under the age of five. In these cases, information about the children's views will often be filtered through their parents, but courts can view separating parents as biased. Allegations of child sexual abuse and domestic violence tend to raise issues of credibility in courts, as we showed in Chapter 7. A woman's fears about abuse may not satisfy a judge that making a contact order could lead to harm to the victim or child. The quality of training that judges have on domestic violence and child sexual abuse will affect the decisions made and possibly their attitudes towards the credibility of women's claims about abuse. The successes found already within newly established specialist domestic violence courts endorse the need for training and for developing some specialisms in practice (Cook *et al.* 2004).

Not all judges, however, can be expected to hold a high degree of specialist knowledge about the research evidence on violence and abuse. This raises questions about how much use judges should make of the advice of experts giving testimony. The tendency to regard women as holding unreasonable fears and unable to focus on the needs of their children has brought a growing reliance on assessments made by experts and evaluators to establish the credibility of allegations of domestic violence. There are also circumstances where the mother may under-estimate the violence and its impact upon the children, and an independent assessment will be needed. This is illustrated in the first case study on page 128, concerning contact for the children, Kelly and May. What weight would be given to the mother's assessment that her children would benefit from seeing a father who had recently subjected her to brutal violence? For whatever reason, the mother may not be aware of or may deny the impact of the domestic violence upon herself and the children. Assessments would be particularly complicated if the violent ex-partner dominated the family's perceptions of the abuse. In our experience, it is rare for courts to question contact if parents appear to agree, but in some situations an independent person's opinion can give a reality check on the level of risk. Clearly, the availability of advocacy for women living with domestic violence will greatly affect the extent to which women feel supported or threatened by courts' attempts to focus realistically on the children's needs.

The growing employment of 'experts' to give testimony on the nature and impact of abuse has brought some positive changes in approach but also new difficulties. The emphasis upon 'expert discourses' on violence in the US (Dobash and Dobash 1992) appears to have been a mixed blessing, allowing more informed responses yet also refining the discrimination between 'deserving' and 'non-deserving' (marginalized minority) victims (Fineman 1989). If access to an expert depends upon access to financial resources to pay legal fees, poorer women will be excluded and will be given second-class justice. On the other hand, having financial resources can aggravate the tendency for a violent ex-partner to extend their abuse to battery by the law. There is no shortage of 'experts' willing to counter feminist research findings and argue the case for fathers' rights. Indeed, New Zealand case law suggests that this trend was established soon after the risk assessment measures were introduced into family law (Radford 2004b). Assessment needs to be rooted in an understanding of the research evidence base which supports a gendered analysis of violence and abuse in the context in which the abuse happens. In the UK, the tragedies resulting from controversial expert testimony about Munchausen Syndrome by Proxy, and the resulting convictions of mothers for child homicide, show the need for accredited training and better post qualifying evaluation of experts. When there is evidence of abuse perpetrated by both parties, knowledge of the research and the gendered context of domestic violence are important for assessing whether or not there was a primary aggressor. Furthermore, without an appreciation of the gendered context, the expert-led approach to domestic violence could become medicalized and focused on alcohol, drug misuse and mental health issues so that assessment of the victim, rather than the violent relationship, will be prioritized (Hester *et al.* 2006).

It is important to consider carefully who assesses the violence, at what stage and then what action is taken as a result. Assessment requires time and resources for adequate staff training. Assessments have to be workable and not over-bureaucratic. Although there is room for developing some specialization in practice, we need to be wary of over-emphasis on experts who could increase conflict in the courts. This requires decisions about what type of assessment might be appropriate. Some issues raised may be particularly complex and need a highly specialist assessment. For others, the assessment may be more straightforward. Training is clearly very important so that those involved in making decisions about who does an assessment have sufficient knowledge to make sound judgements. There are also issues of competence and consistency to consider as a result of the out-sourcing, especially of domestic violence risk assessment on to psychiatric, psychological and voluntary sector services.

## Assessing risk and safety

Risk assessments can help professionals and the courts to make decisions about the safety and value of contact. A risk assessment is a probability calculation that a harmful behaviour or event will occur. This involves an assessment of the frequency of the behaviour/event, its likely impact and whom it will affect (Kemshall 1996). Risk assessment has developed from (at least) two sources – the spread of actuarialism in criminal justice and child protection systems, and the development of risk assessment and safety planning in advocacy and refuge services (Radford, Blacklock and Iwi 2006). Both trends have been heavily influenced by developments in working with violence in the US (Garland 2001; Mullender 1996). The North American approach to risk assessment in contact cases is rooted in a policy response to domestic violence that is substantially dependent upon criminal justice sanctions and the management of dangerous and lethal violence.

Actuarial risk assessment derives from the insurance industry, and it has spread rapidly to statutory agencies concerned to protect themselves from client-initiated court cases for compensation. Actuarial risk assessment draws upon research-based probability calculations to identify the likely level of risk, focusing especially on the most dangerous offender. Its purpose is to manage this risk by containing it and minimizing the likelihood of further harm. Identifying different levels of risk allows practitioners to identify domestic violence and to match the level of risk or need (commonly high, medium or low) to the appropriately targeted level of resources. Risk assessment in criminal justice and child protection have focused mostly on identifying high-risk cases, but good child protection and crime prevention is not just about being vigilant about high-risk cases where someone could die. An over-reliance on risk can divert attention from working constructively to help people solve their problems (Trotter 2004).

In contrast to actuarial risk assessment are the developments based upon safety planning that have evolved within advocacy services and refuges. Here, the purpose of a risk (safety) assessment is to provide knowledge that will assist in safety planning with the victim and children. This differs radically from the actuarial approach because the basic goal is safety and finding ways and resources to help a family achieve this outcome, no matter what the level of risk. Understanding the victim's fears and experiences of living with the violence is a crucial step in getting her better protection. Focusing on safety also means going beyond an assessment of the risk of further physical attack and repeat victimization. Safety includes psychological safety and freedom from fear, creating peace at home. Safety can also be seen to include creating the space to recover from trauma and depression so that continuing confrontation with the triggers for traumatic re-living of the past does not undermine the recovery of both adult and child survivors of domestic violence.

The evidence base for domestic violence risk assessment is growing but is still rather limited. The research literature has drawn conclusions based on:

- Fatality reviews (Websdale 1999) and research conducted in prisons (Soothill *et al.* 2002). These are the atypical and least common cases of domestic violence that result in fatalities or prosecution.

- Victimization and crime surveys (e.g. Walby and Myhill 2002) or reviews of police or agency data (Campbell *et al.* 1998b). The usefulness of these sources depends on what is reported and recorded. Children and young people as victims (or perpetrators) of crime are nearly always absent from crime surveys.

- Surveys of perpetrator characteristics (Gilchrist *et al.* 2003).

Factors commonly linked with a risk of further domestic violence in the research literature include:

- previous physical or sexual assaults (Walby and Myhill 2002)

- an escalation in the frequency and severity of violence (Websdale 1999)

- recent separation (Walby and Myhill 2002)

- either partner's threats and attempts to kill or to commit suicide (Websdale 1999)

- violence in pregnancy (Campbell *et al.* 1998a)

- the perpetrator's possessiveness, jealousy, stalking and psychological abuse of victim

- previous criminality or breach of court orders

- the degree of isolation and vulnerability of the victim. Women aged 16 to 24 report more domestic violence (Walby and Myhill 2002)

- child abuse and previous contact with a child protection agency.

This list is by no means exhaustive, but many of these risk indicators can be found in the various domestic violence risk assessment tools and checklists that now exist (see, for example, the SARA [Spousal Assault Risk Assessment] [Kropp *et al.* 1999] or Campbell's Danger Assessment Checklist [Campbell *et al.* 1998b]).

It is important to note these factors in an assessment although risk assessment can never be wholly accurate nor infallible, or used to predict whether or not an event will happen. Risk assessment procedures cannot guarantee that the outcome will be safety for children and their mothers. Whether or not someone will be safe will depend on a number of factors, including how well the risk assessment is supported by safety planning, risk management and resources. Research on homicides and child deaths has shown that assessments cannot be used to predict even the worst outcomes (Sinclair and Bullock 2002). Searching for 'lethality indicators' can throw up a large number of 'false positives' because indicators of lethality are found in many relationships that do not result in homicide (Kemshall 2002). At the other end of the risk scale, defining a perpetrator of abuse as 'low risk' is not an excuse for complacency. A central pattern in domestic violence is the escalation of abuse. What may be considered 'low risk' initially may change very rapidly – for example, on separation. The process of risk assessment needs to be dynamic and open to review as circumstances can change. The possibility of change can be included up to a point in an assessment. Risk assessments often combine static and dynamic risk factors. Static risk factors focus on the history and past behaviour of the perpetrator and the nature of the past abuse. Dynamic factors consider the changeable characteristics of the perpetrator (such as attitudes) and of the context (such as separation), which can either raise or decrease the risk of further harm. These risk factors need to be understood as being associated with an increased likelihood of further violence rather than as being definitely linked or causal factors. Families and their circumstances are complex and tick-box risk assessments that aggregate numbers to determine how resources and staff are allocated to a case can be too mechanistic to respond appropriately to needs, safety and risk. Some individuals or groups may be more at risk than others as either victims or perpetrators, but stereotyping groups or individuals is unhelpful and discriminatory. Any risk assessment needs to focus on the individuals involved rather than purely on the patterns of abusive relationships. Assessments should not become substitutes for hearing what an individual has to say about her experiences and fears. Assessments also need to be fair and reasonable and able to withstand possible challenges in court.

Assessment needs to be a process rather than a one-off event, with review and monitoring important aspects of improving safety. Key issues for the assessment process in contact cases involving domestic violence are summarized in Box 8.1.

The assessment topics outlined in Box 8.1 are based upon the general argument in this book that the primary focus for decision making should be safety. This means shifting the emphasis away from purely the mother's fears on to the impact of the perpetrator's violence and promoting peace at home

## Box 8.1: Safety and child contact
### – summary of assessment issues

### A. The nature of the violence and level of risk

- Directly ask about the pattern and history of credible allegations of physical, sexual, psychological and financial abuse.

- If there are credible allegations of violence from both parents, can a primary aggressor be identified?

- What is the level of risk? Are there indicators of high risk/lethality and escalating violence? What do static and dynamic indicators suggest?

- Indicators of risk should include any violence in pregnancy, depression, threats/attempts to kill or commit suicide, stalking behaviour, the use of weapons, and the perpetrator's level of proprietariness and sexual jealousy.

- Were others involved or drawn into the violence and abuse by the perpetrator?

- Was there any abuse or neglect of the child?

### B. The impact of the violence on the abused parent

- How has the violence affected the mother's physical, mental and emotional well-being?

- Are there issues that influence the parent's vulnerability to the abuse?

- Assess the degree of isolation and the availability of social support.

- Did the violence affect the mother's ability to protect or shield the child from the abuse?

- How did she cope? What factors supported her efforts to cope and to protect the children?

- How did the violence affect the mother's parenting and relationship with the children?

- What are the mother's fears about further abuse and about contact?

### C. How the violence affected the child

- Was there any abuse or neglect to the child?

- If there was sexual abuse of the child, what was the nature of the perpetrator's 'grooming' and how has this affected the child's relationship with the abusive parent?

- Did the child witness or overhear the violence? How was the child affected?

- Was the child drawn into the abuse?

- How did the child respond to the violence? Did the child hide or withdraw and try to shield him/herself and siblings from the violence? Did the child intervene or adapt his/her behaviour in order to manage the abuser? Did the child act as carer for the mother or siblings?

- Are there any behavioural, developmental or pathological indicators of harm to the child as result of living with the domestic violence?

- What is the nature of the child's bond with the violent parent? To what extent is the bond based upon genuine affection and to what extent is the bond influenced by a traumatic attachment to the violent parent?

- How has the violence affected the child's emotional and psychological safety?

- What were the protective factors – what factors helped the child to cope with living with the domestic violence?

### D. The child's wishes and feelings

- What does the child feel about seeing the father?

- What is the likely risk of harm if contact is granted or refused?

- How would contact affect the child's relationships with siblings?

*Continued on next page*

*Box 8.1 cont.*

### E. The violent parent's motivation and capacity for change

- What is the level of risk posed by the perpetrator's behaviour?

- Are there any drug or alcohol problems?

- Has there been any stalking behaviour?

- What is the level of sexual jealousy/proprietariness?

- Have there been previous breaches of court orders or post-separation harassment? How is the pattern of past/current behaviour likely to be reflected in behaviour on contact visits?

- Does the perpetrator have any empathy for the victim and the children? To what extent is the perpetrator able to understand how his violence affected the mother and child?

- If the perpetrator accepts responsibility for violence, is there any remorse? Is the remorse motivated by his desire for a reconciliation? Have there been previous expressions of remorse and past reconciliations that failed?

- What is the degree of willingness to accept conditions to the contact arrangements and to make amends for past behaviour?

### F. What is safe? Safety arrangements

- What arrangements and what degree of vigilance would be needed to make contact safe?

- Should contact be supervised or just supported? Would limited supervision of 'handover' or even unsupervised contact be safe?

- What would be needed to protect the child's emotional safety and need to have peace at home?

- Would the abused parent feel safe if contact was to supervised by grandparents or other family members? Relatives are usually inappropriate supervisers of contact if there has been domestic violence.

- Safety should be assessed before, during and after any contact.

## G. The quality of contact

- Have there been any previous experiences of contact and how might these affect current arrangements?

- What is the violent parent's capacity to provide worthwhile, caring and interesting contact?

- Is there any need for parenting support?

- Would the violent parent be reliable in attending contact meetings?

- What are the financial implications of contact, especially travel costs, the costs of supervision and monitoring contact?

- What is an appropriate level of frequency for contact?

## H. Indirect contact or no contact?

- Explore the victim's fears about indirect contact.

- What is needed for indirect contact to be safe?

- What information can safely be given to the violent parent?

- What information would be of benefit to the child?

- Would the child's identity and sense of self benefit from life story work and other support with information about the non-resident parent?

## I. Monitoring and moving on

- How will contact be affected by relocation and other changes such as re-marriage?

- What is the best time for holding a review of contact arrangements?

- Re-assess the child's feelings about contact.

- Re-assess the abused parent's fears.

- Is it appropriate to move from supervised contact towards a lower level of safety monitoring? What support is needed for parents wishing to self-manage the contact?

for the mother and child. This involves, as a first step, taking the mother's fears seriously, assessing the nature of the violence, the perpetrator's pattern of behaviour and the resulting risks (addressing the issues covered in A–G in Box 8.1 and discussed in earlier chapters of this book).

## Parenting, fear and trauma

Assessing the impact of the domestic violence upon the child is crucial if children are to be emotionally safe. The assessment especially needs to consider how living with domestic violence may have affected the child's relationship with the violent parent. Attachment theory is based on the belief that children seek closeness with the primary carer as a survival strategy, so that when they face fear they turn to the carer for protection and reassurance. Some attachment theorists argue that abuse and violence negatively affects or disrupts the attachment between the child and the carer/parent because an attachment based mostly on fear creates insecurity and a traumatic bond (Thomas 2005). Bowlby (1982), the leading attachment theorist, noted that infant animals would sometimes attach themselves more strongly to punishing surrogates than to rewarding ones. They often responded to aversive stimuli from parent figures by clinging to them more intensely. This raises the possibility that a child's apparent closeness to the violent parent may be an indicator that the child's relationship has been forged through fear, rather than a sign of a secure attachment based upon affection and security. The traumatic bond is reinforced when an abusive or violent parent switches behaviour between nurturing and terrorizing the child. Parallels have also been drawn between the child's traumatic attachment with a violent parent and the 'Stockholm Syndrome', the term used to refer to hostages' psychological responses to their hostage takers (Herman 2001). In the Stockholm Syndrome, it is a self-preservation strategy for a hostage to adopt a co-operative and supportive stance towards the hostage-taker due to the belief that a captor is less likely to harm a hostage who co-operates. The hostage's need to survive is stronger than their hatred of the captor. Similarly, a child who fears a parent may make efforts to please and appease that parent.

The possibility of there being a traumatic bond between parent and child needs to be considered in cases where children have been exposed to domestic violence. This is especially important if there has been severe abuse witnessed by the children as in some of the case studies at the start of this chapter. Clearly, an assessment of a traumatic bond in these cases is likely to require specialist knowledge about the psychological responses and behaviour of children who have lived with abuse. A traumatic bond could also affect the relationship between the non-abusive parent and the child so that the mother and child could both benefit from parenting support.

## Parenting by violent men

In Chapter 6, we suggested that contact cases are often motivated by the violent man's wish to re-assert control over the ex-partner and the children. It is important that the obsessive desire to maintain control is not mistakenly perceived as being purely an indicator of the father's love and desperation to see his children. Violent fathers may often express love for their children and sorrow at having been parted. Assessments need to consider the perpetrator's motivation in applying for contact, and whether or not the perpetrator has accepted responsibility for the abuse and is genuinely prepared to try to change. It has been argued that perpetrators of abuse and violence should take more responsibility for making contact safe by co-operating with safety plans (keeping injunctions, not harassing ex-partners, etc.), by taking steps to reform and, if means permit, making a financial commitment to the costs of supervision (Jaffe *et al.* 2003).

Perpetrator projects in England and Wales are relatively new developments, few in number and focused more on the minority of men in the criminal justice system than on violent fathers in the family courts. Unlike parenting programmes in the US, Australia and New Zealand, programmes for violent men that focus on their parenting skills are very recent developments in the UK (Humphreys *et al.* 2000; see also programmes offered by the UK group called Fathers Direct). There is scope to develop a more pro-active role to encourage violent fathers to develop parenting skills and more appropriate relationships with their children.

A violent man will generally be a poor role model for his children and may not be a very competent parent (Harne 2004). Mothers' concerns that the father will be an inappropriate role model for the children figure highly among their reasons for not wanting regular contact to be established (Radford *et al.* 1999). Concerns about a father's influence upon boys' attitudes towards risk-taking and aggression can be particularly common as illustrated in the following two examples:

1. Father likes to take risks and gets himself involved in dangerous activities such as rock-climbing and cliff-walking. He believes it is important to use contact visits to expose the children to these activities to 'toughen them up'.

2.   During contact visits, the father arranges fights for his six-year-old son with other boys in his neighbourhood in order to teach him to 'be strong'.

The first example illustrates the importance of assessing the father's parenting in the context of the circumstances of the particular family.

Courts in the US, Australia and New Zealand have been given powers to mandate parenting programme attendance for a violent parent when custody or contact issues are being considered. It seems likely that these powers to refer to parenting programmes will at some stage be introduced into English family courts. There has, however, been little research into the effectiveness of these programmes for improving the safety of women and children, and in sustaining relationships which are of value for children. How long might it take to rehabilitate a violent parent? Indeed, is it possible, given the findings of high drop-out rates and limited successes from evaluations of domestic violence perpetrator programmes (Burton, Regan and Kelly 1998; Edleson and Tolman 1992)? By 2003, a National Institute of Justice report noted that over 35 studies of perpetrator programmes had been conducted in the US, but it was still not possible to conclude whether or not the programmes had any effect (Jackson *et al.* 2003). As the report concludes, more research is needed to investigate which types of interventions work in which circumstances for which individuals. In support of perpetrator programmes, it could be argued that their success depends greatly upon what they are realistically expected to achieve. Changing the behaviour of violent men and sustaining this change over the long term is more difficult to achieve and to support with empirical evidence than an improvement to the safety of the victims. A more readily measurable indicator of success would be whether the efforts of perpetrator and parenting programmes to challenge and contain the man's violent behaviour improve the safety of the woman and children. The shift towards parenting plans and providing more parenting support provides an opportunity for the safety and workability of contact arrangements to be considered. It is crucial that policy and practice draw upon evidence about what works in order to counter the campaigns of misinformation and inaccuracies which have unfortunately been so well publicized by more extreme elements of the father's rights movement.

## Supervising contact

Courts are increasingly relying upon contact or child visitation centres to provide a safe venue for children to meet with the non-resident parent. The availability of supervised contact services to protect women and children from domestic violence is nonetheless limited. Generally, professional supervision will be limited to a period of assessment and then there will be a move towards less vigilant supervision, often by relatives of one of the parents. There is a great lack of clarity about the meaning of the word 'supervision', and a degree of optimism about its potential to enhance the welfare of children who have contact with violent fathers. 'Supervision' in England has often been confused with 'supported contact' where no actual supervision occurs at all. 'Supervision' can range from direct one-to-one overseeing and monitoring of interactions between parent and child to maintaining a presence in a room full of parents and their children. 'Supervision' might also be seen to mean having contact at a relative's house, without the relative necessarily being in the same room as the child and parent throughout the visit. Supervision by family members is seldom appropriate when there has been domestic violence, because the supervisors may collude with or find themselves threatened or implicated in the abuse of the mother (Hester and Radford 1996a, and see Chapter 5). Children are also less safe. The AMICA (Aid for Mothers Involved in Contact Applications) research found that half the children who had contact supervised by family members were said to have been abused during contact visits (Radford *et al.* 1999), and instances from the contact study were cited in Chapter 5.

In some parts of North America, Australia and New Zealand, contact centres have firmly emphasized safety. Vigilance over security is necessary but it cannot guarantee safety. It is difficult, for instance, to guarantee that a child will not be snatched or harmed. What degree of security and vigilance would be acceptable for a service concerned with the welfare of children?

With direct supervision or professional overseeing of contact, it may be less likely that children will be physically or sexually abused. Supervision may not, however, prevent emotional abuse, especially the 'mind control' forms, or the father's priming of the child for further sexual abuse. In these circumstances, there is a danger that establishing supervision might make it appear to the child that the abuse or sexual violence was condoned. It could be argued that face-to-face contact will generally be inappropriate unless the child has had some therapeutic help and a chance to overcome some of the effects of abuse. This would be so particularly where children show signs of post-traumatic stress as a result of experiencing or witnessing violence. It is also often the case that full knowledge of the abuser's tactics to control or 'groom' a child will not have come to light by the time contact is set up, raising difficult questions about the extent to which contact centres need to assess and monitor visitation sessions, and explore what sort of relationship is being preserved for the child.

Independent evaluations of supervised visitation services have found that women feel safer and less fearful when the child's contact is properly supervised (Strategic Partners Pty Ltd 1998). In an evaluation of government-sponsored supervised contact services in Australia, three-quarters of the 49 children studied over a 12-month period said they felt safer. Most children had improved relationships with the non-resident parent after three months. The substantial behavioural and emotional disturbances, which the children showed at the start of contact, subsided over time. The children's recovery appears to have been strongly linked to the mother's safety and well-being while using the service (Strategic Partners Pty Ltd 1998). Another Australian study of children living in shelters however found impressive recovery patterns for children who had *no contact* with their fathers or who were unafraid of them (Mertin 1995). Clearly, it is crucial for the recovery of women and children that the fear of domestic violence is reduced.

While some children feel safer, research in England found that a significant minority of children remained fearful about meeting their fathers at contact centres (Humphreys and Harrison 2003). There has been little debate as to how actively contact centres should promote contact. Taking a positive attitude and providing a welcoming environment is generally viewed as good practice for contact centre workers. However, to what extent should contact centre workers encourage an apprehensive child to meet a father? If the child's reluctance is based on fear or possibly undisclosed abuse, encouragement to meet the father would be abusive. What do centres do about the compliant but fearful child? Working with the child's reluctance in this way further presents difficulties in assessing whether or not contact is likely to become viable at a later stage if efforts to support it are maintained. The 'short term harm' thinking, which has dominated English court decisions, endorses contact centres' optimism about the value of contact. It may be straightforward to agree that a cessation of contact is needed if abusive behaviour is witnessed by a contact centre worker on centre premises, but how is the ongoing value of contact to be assessed otherwise? What about the child who is having nightmares and is bedwetting at home but seems to cope with contact at the centre? What signs of distress in the child are relevant indicators that s/he may not be getting any benefit from contact?

An assumption which underpins the contact centre movement is the idea of providing a service which will rehabilitate relationships between parents to the point where contact can become self-managed and the centre's involvement redundant. Little is known about *how* centres strive to move parents towards self-managed contact arrangements, and in England and Wales this may be little more than putting a time limit on the family's use of the centre. There may be greater problems in evaluating the value of contact to a child if a contact centre provides help only with arranging the exchange of children between parents who otherwise have contact unsupervised or supervised by family or friends. The American writers Garrity and Baris (1995) argue for a therapeutic approach, which focuses on the needs of the particular child to have psychological and physical safety, and which progresses, at the child's pace, to 'parenting recovery'. Evaluation studies are needed to test the success of this approach.

Although it appears that carefully supervised visits between children and a violent parent can be set up so that some children and mothers feel safe, there are no research studies as yet showing any longer term benefits to children from contact with a violent parent. Clearly, more research is needed to justify both the continued commitment to preserving children's contact with violent parents and the substantial financial investment put into supervised contact services. The main conclusion to be drawn from the contact research is that it is presently inconclusive. When setting up contact between children and *violent* fathers, courts are embarking on experiments where the impact upon the welfare of children is uncertain.

## Conclusion

The main issue we have stressed in this chapter is the need to include considerations of domestic violence and child safety in family court assessments in child contact cases. We have tried to stress the importance of assessing the specific needs of children in the context of their family relationships, taking into account how relationships may have been affected by the trauma associated with living with abuse. If contact is to serve the interests of children, then there needs to be a willingness to challenge the dogmatic belief that children's welfare is nearly always best supported by preserving contact with a biological parent.

# From Blaming Mothers to Providing Positive Support – The Role of Welfare Agencies

As argued in previous chapters, the tendency by the courts and legal professionals to construe women as the problem in child contact cases, rather than the men who are violent, creates situations where both women and children continue to be abused. Yet, supporting mothers to be safe has been recognized as a particularly positive approach in child protection where domestic violence is an issue. So what is the problem? A major problem faced by practitioners working with mothers and children experiencing domestic violence is that they are presented with a set of quite different, separate and indeed contradictory ideas and practice approaches in relation to 'domestic violence', 'child protection' and 'child contact' respectively. Mothers and fathers end up construed quite differently in relation to 'safe parenting' and mother blaming is the outcome. In this chapter, these issues and the consequences for practitioners from welfare agencies and organizations working with domestic violence are discussed, and we look at how some professionals have managed to move away from woman blaming to the use of more supportive and positive approaches.

## Child protection and domestic violence – development of services

In both North America and the UK, services dealing with child maltreatment and protection developed separately from those dealing with domestic violence. This has meant that child protection professionals and services have often ignored women's experiences of domestic violence and the work carried out by refuges and other organizations dealing with this issue. The theorizing of woman abuse and child abuse have similarly developed along different lines. As Stark and Flitcraft document for the US, feminist thinking has been influential in developing understanding of domestic violence as gendered – as a crime carried out by men and rooted in sexual inequality (1996, p.73). Increasing police intervention backed by legal approaches has been the result of this criminalization of domestic violence (see Chapter 1). Child maltreatment and abuse can also be explained through the feminist-informed model, but such abuse has instead tended to be explained through recourse to ideas about family dysfunction or pathology. Rather than a criminalizing of child maltreatment and abuse, such pathologizing has led to an emphasis on child welfare interventions where mothers in particular are seen as culpable although fathers are the abusers (Armstrong 2000). While there have been developments in recent years in family welfare practice where child protection takes into account issues for children and impacts of domestic violence, the tension between the different understandings of domestic violence and child abuse continues to be discernible.

Similarly in the UK, legal, professional and family policy discourses have tended to present violence against women and violence against children as two separate areas, with different explanations and different professional approaches (Hester *et al.* 2006). As in the US, the UK has seen increasing criminalization of domestic violence, while an apparent *de*-criminalization has taken place as regards child abuse via a welfare approach that emphasizes 'partnership with parents' (Hester *et al.* 2006). These different and diverging areas have led to often contradictory policy and practice where social work responses concerning children have emphasized mothers' responsibility for their own and their children's safety while ignoring violent men. The safety of mothers, and their children, has been undermined (Hester *et al.* 2006; Humphreys 2000).

A further divide can be identified in child care policy between child protection and professional practice on parental separation. Despite increasing recognition that child maltreatment should be considered when decisions are made about custody, visitation and contact (see also Chapter 4), Jaffe *et al.* (2001) suggest in relation to North America that:

> most domestic violence advocates would probably describe a significant gap between theory and practice when it comes to recognising domestic violence as a pertinent factor in custody determinations and affording due consideration to maternal and child safety. (p.191)

Similarly in the UK, in the Children Act 1989 – the legislation covering both child protection and arrangements for children after parental divorce or separation – parents are construed very differently. Child protection is underpinned by a notion that parents may be harmful and abusive to children, with social workers ready to intervene on behalf of the state. As we argued in Chapter 7, the law's approach to parental separation relies instead on a much more positive construct of parents as good for children, able to communicate and to negotiate contact arrangements. This division becomes particularly acute in situations where a separating or divorcing father has been abusive to a child.

## Life on three planets

The professional approaches to domestic violence, child protection, and visitation and contact are so different that they may be conceived as belonging to different planets. The result is the story of Planet A, Planet B and Planet C (see Figure 9.1) (Hester 2004).

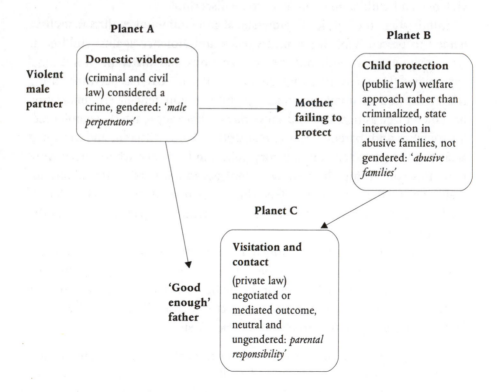

*Figure 9.1: Three planet model*

The three planets each have their own history, culture and laws. On Planet A – the domestic violence planet – the father's behaviour may be recognized by the police and other agencies as abusive in relation to the mother; his behaviour is seen as a crime and he may even be prosecuted for a criminal or public order offence. He might also have a restraining or protective order taken out against him. He is thus perceived as a *violent partner* and the woman in need of protection. If, instead, he arrives on Planet B – the child protection planet – he may also be perceived as abusive to the mother while the parents are still together or during the process of their separating. But the focus of Planet B is on protecting children not adults. His abuse of the mother may lead to the involvement in the family of social services, and result in the children being placed on the child protection register for emotional abuse. It is highly unlikely, however, that he will be prosecuted on Planet B because a predominantly welfare, rather than criminalizing, approach prevails. In order to protect the children, social workers are likely to insist instead that the mother removes herself and her children from his presence, and leaves the relationship if she has not already done so. If she does not, then it is she who is seen as 'failing to protect', and the children might be removed into the care of the local authority. On Planet B, therefore, despite the violence to the mother being from the male partner, it is the *mother who is seen as responsible* for dealing with the consequences. In effect, the violent man disappears out of the picture. From Planet B or Planet A, the father moves to Planet C – the visitation and contact planet – in order to apply for contact with his children. As there has been no prosecution of him on Planet B in relation to the emotional abuse of the children that resulted from his violence to the mother (despite their being on the child protection register for this), there is no apparent 'concrete' evidence in relation to child care to question his post-separation parenting abilities. Even if he has a criminal conviction or protection order against him as a result of his violence against the mother on Planet A, this may still be seen as 'between the adults' and not directly related to the children. On Planet C, the emphasis is less on protection than on children having two parents. Within this context, an abusive father may still be deemed a *'good enough'* father, who should have at least contact with his child post-separation if not custody or residence. The mother ends up in a particularly difficult dilemma on Planet C. She has attempted to curb his violent behaviour by calling the police and supporting his prosecution on Planet A. She has left her violent partner following instruction from social services on Planet B that she leave in order to protect her children. However, Planet C in effect has the opposite approach – that families should continue to be families even if there is divorce and separation.

On Planet C, she is therefore ordered to allow contact between her violent partner and the children, leaving her not only bewildered and confused but also yet again scared for the safety of her children. As we showed in Chapter 7, realistic assessment of risk and lethality for children is extremely difficult within such a context.

The 'three planets' model also shows that there is a conceptual gap between 'violent men' on the one hand and 'fathers' on the other (Eriksson and Hester 2001; Hester 2004). There are violent men but 'good enough' fathers, and the two are difficult to merge whether in policy or practice.

In the following sections, we look at some of the policy responses to Hester's (2004) 'three planets' issues, and examine the problems arising in the practice of child welfare agencies on Planet B in particular.

## Trying to support but blaming mothers

As we discussed in Chapter 2, research on women, children and domestic violence indicates how both the physical and emotional effects of the domestic violence can for some women have a detrimental impact on their mothering and relationships with their children. Mothers experiencing domestic violence may therefore appear as inadequate or unable to cope. However, with support, and in particular with help to be safe, mothers are generally able to resume parenting of their children. Holden *et al.* (1998) found significant improvements in women's parenting six months after separation if the partner's violence had been stemmed.

In recent years, there have been attempts in welfare policy and practice to move in this direction and thus to move away from the problems identified by the 'three planets', in particular Planet B, in relation to mothers seen as 'failing to protect'. Supporting mothers to be safe from violent men has been increasingly recognized as a positive approach in child protection, originally in the US and echoed in English policy directives (DH 1997b). For example, in England, the Department of Health issued guidance in relation to the Family Law Act 1996 suggesting that:

> [w]here domestic violence may be an important element in the family, the safety of [usually] the mother is also in the child's welfare [sic] (DH 1997b p.12).

Such an approach also fits with the new emphasis in England on 'children in need' which allows local authorities to provide a range of support to children and their non-abusive carers – including assisting women and their children after the abuser has been removed, or supporting women and children to leave violent men (DH 1999; see also Chapter 4).

However, in practice, neither the courts nor welfare practitioners are generally applying this approach, and the problems identified in Hester's (2004) 'three planets' model remain. Jaffe *et al.* (2003), discussing the North American juvenile courts, cite numerous cases of mothers losing their parental rights due to a perceived failure to protect their children from abusive partners, while abusive men are still being perceived as 'good enough' parents and even being given custodial rights. Jaffe *et al.* (2003) express particular concern about instances where the child has witnessed abuse of the mother by her male partner/child's father, but where it is the mother whose parental rights are terminated. For instance:

> in *In re Lonell J* (N.Y. App. Div., 1998), 973 N.Y.S.2d 116, in which the battered mother was found to have emotionally neglected her children because they witnessed her being abused by the father, in spite of evidence that police were called repeatedly, the father was arrested, and a protective order was issued. (Jaffe *et al.* 2003, p.103)

And similarly:

> in the *Matter of Deandre T.* (N.Y. App. Div. 1998), 253 A.D.2d 497, the father's abuse of the mother in front of one of their children was sufficient to sustain a finding of neglect of that child's sibling. (Jaffe *et al.* 2003, p.103)

Although some such cases have been reversed on appeal, the general trend remains. The authors conclude that, although phrases such as 'witnessing domestic violence is child abuse' are useful to draw attention to the interlinking of woman and child abuse, they should be used with caution. If witnessing domestic violence is seen as child abuse, women experiencing domestic violence will continue to be accused of 'secondary abuse' or having 'engaged in domestic violence' (Jaffe *et al.* 2003, pp.101–2).

In our Barnardos study (Hester and Scott 2000), social workers and health visitors interviewed said they were keen to support mothers. The agencies, while offering a variety of support also appeared to expect a lot from the women. As one of the women explained, it is especially difficult to function, both physically and emotionally, in the aftermath of a violent incident. It is almost an 'out of body' experience, in which both your body and mind are numbed. Nonetheless it was often precisely at these moments that they were expected to take in information from agencies and invariably 'protect' the children from any further violence or abuse. Clearly, the women did have their own safety strategies, but had usually contacted the agencies because they had had enough and needed others to take some of the load. However, although social services would provide child care respite sessions and support with parenting, there was little evidence that they were using the DH-sanctioned approach of focusing on mother's safety as a means of enabling child protection. There appeared to be little work specifically involving safety strategies or safety planning being used to create safety for the women and consequently for the children. In many respects, therefore, the onus was still on the women to ensure their own (and their children's) safety, and for social services in particular this served as proof of a woman's ability to protect her children. However, without emphasizing and ensuring women's safety and freedom from violence, the underlying problem which women and children in domestic violence situations face – the male partners'/fathers' violence – was not dealt with. It became easier to end up blaming women for failing to protect their children, as happened to some of the women. For instance, one of the women in the research group had previously lost her children into care because she was reluctant to leave her abusive partner, and a case conference involving social services and other agencies concerning one of the other women had made veiled threats to remove her children (see also Humphreys 1997).

## Violent men but good fathers

Parenting involves both mothers and fathers, and parenting by violent and abusive fathers also needs to be taken into account. Research by Holden and Ritchie (1991) in the US found that children were more likely to have to cope with negative fathering from the domestic violence perpetrator than other children. In their study of women and children in shelters and a comparison group of women, the violent men were reported as being more irritable, less involved in child rearing, less physically affectionate, and used more negative control techniques such as physical punishment than men in the comparison group. In our study of child contact arrangements, fathers were often reported to lack parenting skills or interest in caring for children, leading in some instances to dangerous or even deadly situations for the children concerned (Hester and Radford 1996a). Yet, professionals were found to be very optimistic about men's parenting skills, while scrutinizing women's parenting in much greater detail. This has also been echoed in Farmer and Owen's (1995) study of child protection outcomes, and Jaffe *et al.*'s (2003) review of US juvenile court cases.

In our Barnardos study (Hester and Scott 2000), the fathers continued to be involved in some way with the children in four out of six families. They would be in and out of the households, perhaps living there for short periods but also excluded via restraining or protective orders following their violence against the women, or because they had moved on to another relationship. Yet, apart from the police, none of the professionals had much if any contact with the fathers or stepfathers. All the women had children on the social services child protection register or social services involvement because of the men's violent and abusive behaviour. As indicated earlier, there was also a general expectation, from social services in particular, that the women should leave their violent partners in order to protect their children. Nonetheless the men were in most instances seen as having some part to play as parents, and were at times perceived (less critically) as better parents than the women. Echoing the 'gap' between violent men and men as fathers that we identified earlier, there was a similar separation by professionals interviewed of the men's abusive behaviour and their ability to parent:

> I think I saw him probably twice, and he has much better ideas about parenting, like you know, if you tell them you're going to do something you do it, and you follow it through…he obviously cared about the children… (Health visitor)

But this man was also violent and behaved inappropriately in front of the children, and the children were placed on the child protection register largely because of this:

> And he would get very angry and he'd start shouting at her… And then there'd be a big argument, and the children witnessing this…talking about lots of things that were really inappropriate…it would have been better if he'd kept it and talked about it afterwards. (Health visitor)

It was apparent from interviews with both the mothers and the social workers that male partners would use their supposedly better 'fathering' against the women. In particular, the men would use talk of how they could do parenting better in order to put down their female partners. By not dealing critically with the men's violent behaviour and dissociating it from their parenting, some of the welfare agencies thus ended up colluding with the men's abusive behaviour against the women. Despite most of the men's ongoing involvement with the children, no-one appeared to be addressing their parenting abilities.

## Violent men becoming more visible?

Recent policy debates have recognized that women and children should not necessarily be the ones to leave their home, schools, friends, etc. where the partner/father is violent. With regard to welfare agencies, there are provisions in the Family Law Act 1996 which increase the powers of social services to oust abusers. Under the previous Children Act 1989 guidance (vol. 1, para. 4.31) social workers were encouraged to remove the abuser rather than the child from the family home, wherever possible, although in practice this was difficult (DH 1997a). The Family Law Act 1996 has amended the Children Act 1989 so that this approach is strengthened (s.52 of, and Schedule 6 to, the Family Law Act 1996, amendment to the Children Act 1989, s.38 and s.44). In addition, under schedule 2, paragraph 5 of the Children Act 1989, social services can offer financial assistance to enable the abuser to pay for alternative accommodation.

In practice however, there have been very few instances where this legislation has been used by social services, thereby indicating that social workers still prefer or find it easier to target women rather than violent men (Hester and Westmarland 2005). Similarly, in our Barnardos study, none of the child care or health professionals surveyed were aware of the new provisions (Hester and Scott 2000). Dealing with the men on the basis of the domestic violence was deemed much more difficult than working with the mothers, and workers were unclear as to whether prosecution or removal of the men from the scene was indeed useful. One social worker, for instance, was concerned that the issuing of a protective order against the man had prevented her from working with the man and woman together. She saw the criminalizing of the man's behaviour as interfering directly with her welfare and partnership-oriented approach, even if that was not containing his violence either and meant that the woman had to be in same room as her ex-partner:

> I can't see them together if there's an injunction out. If there are legal things or proceedings in, enormous, then I can't help them, this has impeded work with them, with the both of them, because obviously I can't override that and say, 'OK, well let's meet', and we've had to cancel one or two meetings… (Social worker)

Using a multi-agency approach, with meetings and service level agreements with a range of other agencies, and 'panels' to discuss intransigent cases and to plan a more comprehensive approach involving safety of the mother, protection of the child *and* restraint of the abusive father, would have been a much more positive approach in this instance (see Hester and Westmarland 2005).

## Developing positive practice

In recent years, the evidence base of 'what works' to support women experiencing domestic violence has been growing (Taylor-Browne 2001). In England and Wales, for example, the Home Office funded a range of crime reduction initiatives on domestic violence that have been independently evaluated. These included the work of child care and welfare agencies (Hester and Westmarland 2005). The evaluation studies plus our own earlier work provide examples of how practitioners may overcome some of the problems inherent in the contradictory and woman-blaming framework underlying the 'three planets' approaches, and instead provide positive support to mothers and their children. We cannot provide a comprehensive review of the work here, but in the rest of this chapter we will focus on a few useful approaches.

In the Home Office initiative, 29 domestic violence projects were evaluated over periods of one to two years (Hester and Westmarland 2005). Overwhelmingly, the research echoed earlier indications that a multi-agency approach is crucial and has to underpin any work by welfare or other agencies engaged in work with families experiencing domestic violence (Hague and Malos 1996; Home Office 2000; Humphreys *et al.* 2000; James-Hanman 2000). Only a multi-agency approach can deal with the complexities of domestic violence. Only a multi-agency approach can begin to overcome the problems highlighted by the 'three planets' model by incorporating agencies from each of the different 'planets' and creating joint policies and practices. We do not want to go into more detail about the mechanisms or processes of multi-agency working here as useful guides already exist (Hague and Malos 1996; Hague, Mullender and Aris 2004). Just to summarize, the more effective multi-agency strategies ensured that the issues of confidentiality and referral processes were clarified, including the sharing of data; that policies were consistent within and between agencies; that there was full and active involvement of the women's shelter or refuge and outreach services as well as domestic violence survivors; and that there were measurable improvements in resources.

In this chapter, we will focus on two other aspects of relevance to welfare agencies:

1.  How agencies involved in child protection may incorporate domestic violence in their work to ensure that a supportive and positive, rather than punitive and mother-blaming, approach results. This will draw on our NSPCC research (Hester and Pearson 1998).

2.  How welfare agencies may use routine enquiry coupled with an understanding of power and control to empower women and move from a woman blaming to a supportive approach. This will draw on the Home Office evaluations of social work and health visitors' practice (Hester and Westmarland 2005).

## Incorporating domestic violence in child protection work

The NSPCC research involved working with an NSPCC team and examining their incorporation of domestic violence as an issue for both mothers and children in their work with abused children. The NSPCC is the only organization in the UK other than social services to have a statutory duty to protect children from harm. The team involved in the research were working within the tradition and practice of child protection (the practice on Planet B) outlined earlier in this chapter, but were seeking to overcome the distinctions between Planet A (the domestic violence planet) and Planet B.

Two main approaches were adopted:

1.  Use of team meetings to discuss definitions of domestic violence, and to examine the incorporation of domestic violence through 're-framing' of past and current cases.

2.  The development of a simple monitoring scheme for domestic violence to be applied across the team's work.

From the onset it was important to agree on a definition of domestic violence with the team which could be used in the project. The definition adopted reflected the experiences described by women in such situations, and outlined in Chapters 1 and 2 in this book, with an emphasis on the controlling aspects and the belief that psychological abuse may have as much, or more, impact as physical abuse (Dobash and Dobash 1980; Hester and Radford 1996a; Kelly 1988).

In order to explore the use of a 'domestic violence focused' framework in the team's work, some of the team meetings were used to re-examine and *re-frame* certain cases. Previously closed cases where we as researchers had identified domestic violence but where this had not been made apparent or explicit by the NSPCC team, or where its existence remained as a possibility in the background, were brought to the team for discussion. This re-framing exercise involved the exploration of the effect that taking domestic violence into account might have had on each individual case. In this way, domestic violence was used as one of the 'lenses' through which to look at the practice which was carried out. The use of 're-framing' to incorporate domestic violence proved a very useful mechanism for the integration of work around both child abuse and domestic violence. As one team member explained, it was this re-examination of cases which had proved a very useful approach to examining alternative practice possibilities, and, in particular, had clarified for her how the 'domestic violence lens' could enhance her work with children:

> the thing that brought it home to me was that session we had when we looked at some cases, we traced the domestic violence, we traced the problems back…and it sort of really brought it home to me that there we all were, all the different agencies, running round in circles basically trying to help families, not actually considering the issue of the domestic violence and how problems that had either arisen from that or been exacerbated by that, and that in fact we probably had to go back and deal with that domestic violence issue to make any headway at all…to be able to benefit from some therapy and get their lives back on course. (quoted in Hester 2000, p.105)

Discussing cases in this way emphasized to the team the need to put child protection concerns into the domestic violence framework, and to look at the impact of domestic violence on the child in a much broader context.

By focusing on domestic violence as a possible issue, and beginning to ask mothers and (to a lesser extent) children referred to the NSPCC about possible experiences of domestic violence, the existence of domestic violence in the lives of children who had been abused became increasingly visible. By the end of the project (and as already indicated in Chapters 4 and 5) it was apparent that two-thirds of the cases accepted for service by the NSPCC team also involved domestic violence (virtually always violence against the mother by her male partner); also, that the perpetrator of the domestic violence and the abuser of the child(ren) was likely to be the same individual, usually the child's natural father. There was much evidence of the generally abusive impact on children, both 'indirect' and 'direct', of living in circumstances of domestic violence. For the team, being made aware of these patterns in the cases they dealt with helped them to work more realistically with children and their mothers where domestic violence was also a part of their experience. Realizing that for some children their abuser was also violent to the mothers, and vice versa, led to greater understanding of the abusive dynamics experienced by the children concerned. It also meant that in the few instances where mothers contacted the NSPCC regarding support for their children who had lived in circumstances of domestic violence, team members became more open to the possibility that the children had been directly abused, in addition to witnessing violence to their mothers.

Examples of narrative taken from each of the team's case files in the period before and after the team began to incorporate domestic violence provided further evidence of how the issue of domestic violence was moving from the periphery to becoming a more central and integrated feature of the work undertaken by the team as the project progressed. In the case files in the period prior to the project began, the existence of domestic violence might be acknowledged by the team, but tended not to be explored in the work undertaken with the child, as exemplified by the following case file extract:

> [girl child, 11] expressed negative feelings towards her father and was concerned about episodes of violence in her birth family... I [NSPCC worker] am still unsure as to the nature and extent of the domestic difficulties which she [child] experienced in her birth family.

In this instance, the child expressed anxiety in the initial NSPCC session about 'her dad hitting her mum', but this disappeared from subsequent sessions where the focus was on the presenting issue of the sexual abuse of the child by the father. The complexities and impact of the child's abusive experiences within the context of domestic violence were not addressed, and the worker did not attempt to gain details and information from the child to clarify the 'nature and extent of the domestic difficulties'. Domestic violence and the abuse of the child tended, thus, to be seen as separate issues.

During the first year of the project, more examples of domestic violence being incorporated into the work with the child concerned were apparent. For instance:

> Mrs Green explained that when she was about 17 she had a partner who was violent towards her. Daisy [daughter now aged 11] was aged two at the time. Daisy said that she could remember instances from that time... Daisy has informed Mrs Green that she has nightmares about her early years when Mrs Green had a violent partner... Mrs Green and Daisy...talked about how a violent relationship that Mrs Green was in when Daisy was one or two years old had impacted on both of them.

In this instance, the presenting issue was again child sexual abuse, but there was much more readiness by the NSPCC staff to use the sessions also to explore past issues relating to domestic violence and to acknowledge the continuing impact of this for both mother and daughter. In this way, channels of communication were opened up between mother and daughter, and Daisy's current difficulties could be located within a wider context.

By the end of the project, acknowledgement of the inter-connectedness of domestic violence and the safety and welfare of the child became much more clearly integrated into practice. For example, in one case accepted by the team, the presenting issue for the child, as reported by the mother, was the need to explore issues relating to the domestic violence the child had witnessed (rather than child sexual or physical abuse as in earlier cases). Exploring these issues then led to the discovery of the direct physical and sexual abuse of the child by her father:

> Mrs Blue discussed that Lily [daughter aged 11] had witnessed the violence towards her mum. She [Lily] was threatened verbally and physically and was assaulted physically and verbally by her father... Lily has told [Mum] that she doesn't love her dad, but pretended to, to stop him from hurting Mrs Blue... Lily has nightmares, cannot handle aggression in any form... Cannot bear anyone to touch her.

Addressing the violence in this way, therefore, led to a greater awareness of the issues for the child in coping with the impact of both the direct abuse and the witnessing of abuse associated with living in the context of domestic violence. It also led to a greater awareness of the dynamics of the relationship between Lily and her mother, leading to more effective intervention with them both.

By the end of the project, there had been a clear change within the team, both in relation to awareness of domestic violence issues and in relation to the team's practice. Crucially, there was a change from usually seeing domestic violence as a separate issue from children and child abuse to seeing it as a possibly central issue for children, and as a part of their abusive experiences. Thinking about both child abuse and domestic violence had allowed the team to reflect more thoroughly on their use of particular approaches, largely because many of the underlying dynamics and issues were the same or overlapped. Both domestic violence and child abuse involve one person (often the same individual) exerting power and control over another. The team felt that routinely asking about domestic violence had been very important to their practice. Overall, the project had enabled the team to incorporate domestic violence as part of the picture in working with abused children and their families, leading to much greater emphasis on safety and more effective work with both women and children.

## Understanding power and control

One of the 29 domestic violence projects funded by the Home Office and evaluated as part of the Violence Against Women initiative was the Suffolk

Tools for Practitioners (TfP) project (Hester and Westmarland 2005). The project was evaluated over a two-year period. A local consultation with women experiencing domestic violence had indicated a lack of consistent safety-oriented responses by local agencies, and that danger signs were often ignored with women not being asked about experiences related to domestic violence. The TfP project set out to remedy this by developing 'tools' that practitioners could use for routine enquiry (or 'screening') to enable women to disclose domestic violence and allow early intervention; and safety and crisis planning tools to use with those who did disclose. The screening tools involved a set of questions that practitioners might ask and could tailor to their own needs. The safety and crisis planning tools had checklists to discuss with women regarding information, important items and anything else they would need to have to hand in case of further abusive incidents. There were also booklets with key questions and information for the women themselves. The tools were used by health visitors and social workers, and helped the practitioners using them to support women in relation to the abuse they were experiencing from partners, and also in their role as mothers. Like the NSPCC research, the TfP project thus helped to bring together the two previously separate areas of domestic violence (Planet A) and child protection (Planet B).

The TfP tools were underpinned by the approach created by the domestic violence programme in Duluth, Minnesota. The Duluth approach has at its centre the safety and empowerment of victims as well as accountability of perpetrators. It emphasizes that domestic violence involves 'power over' victims and 'control by' perpetrators, with a generally gendered approach being employed. The Duluth approach incorporates a number of 'wheels' that show the dynamics of domestic abuse, including the 'power and control' and 'equality' wheels, which were used in the TFP project (for information and to see these wheels, go to www.duluth-model.org).

Practitioners wanting to use the tools took part in a three-stage training programme:

1. multi-agency training on awareness of domestic violence

2. team based training on tools use

3. review sessions.

Involvement in all three stages was crucial to the successful implementation of the tools.

The interviews with the health visitors in the early stages of implementation indicated that the tools fitted well with their existing practice approach which included review sessions and interviews with new and about-to-be mothers. Their focus on mothers, use of systematic inventories and questions such as the Edinburgh Post-Natal Depression Inventory lent themselves well to the introduction of screening questions. Screening also fitted with the early intervention strategy they were expected to adopt. The health visitors therefore found it relatively easy to use the screening questions routinely.

Interviews with the same health visitors a year later indicated that they had increasingly seen incorporation of domestic violence screening as an important part of their work. They were all enthusiastic and very positive about having incorporated screening and safety planning into their work. Whereas a year ago they expressed insecurity and anxiety about asking about domestic violence, now they were relaxed about it and saw it as an obvious and useful shift in their practice. This also fitted with the general shift they were expected to make in their practice to focusing on families and not just mother/child. They had developed their own ways of asking about domestic violence, usually at the ante-natal visit and at the six-week visit after the birth of the child. Asking had become a natural aspect of the questions they asked. They were picking up that there may be domestic violence in instances where previously they would not have thought about it or would have accepted a woman's explanation of having walked into a door/falling, etc. The number of domestic violence incidents identified by the health visitors had more than doubled. They felt better equipped to deal with disclosures themselves and to know when and where to refer women on.

In interviews, the health visitors talked about how they had shifted their practice from woman blaming to empowering women, by understanding the dynamics of domestic violence and, in particular, beginning to understand why women 'do not just leave'. The aspect of the tools which the health visitors (and social care staff) found particularly useful by the end of the evaluation was the Duluth wheels – both the power and control and the equality wheels. The wheels were important in showing the nature and dynamics of domestic violence, and they were able to use the wheels directly with women to help them identify that they were in abusive relationships, as well as enabling early intervention and prevention:

> You know there's one case I had recently…a case conference was called because there's an injured child. And we believe it was a violent stepfather. And she denied everything. And it was very good when we went to case conference and in two weeks she actually got rid of him and she said there was a couple of things that made her realize. One was the equality [wheel]. I had asked her, 'you look at this. Where do you fit in?' And she said, 'it suddenly became clear to me.' And that was very positive. She was able to identify

> herself in that relationship. I mean she's taken the wheel and said, 'I'm going to use that for future partners.' (Hester 2006, p.105)

The health visitors were also in a position to enable disclosure where other agencies were unable to do so. In one instance, where domestic violence was suspected, the child was found to be sitting in a pile of glass and social care became involved. The mother did not trust social care services but allowed the health visitor to use the tools (specifically the screening questions and Duluth wheels) with her. Following this work, there were no repeat incidents of domestic violence and the mother had also understood the dangers to the child.

Social services staff also found that use of the tools improved their practice with the families they worked with. They had systematized the use of screening by incorporating this into the initial assessment that they conducted when mothers were first in contact with them. Over a one-year period, the number of disclosures of domestic violence had more than trebled. Screening had also increased in situations where domestic violence was not already known to have occurred. In some instances, they were following up disclosures using the safety planning tool and/or Duluth wheels. One of the social workers interviewed talked about how pleasantly surprised she was that people responded quite openly when asked about domestic violence. The extent of domestic violence was also greater than she had anticipated:

> And I actually think that people are more, are more open to discussing it than I initially thought they would. I think because you raise it, they are actually more open to talk about it than I thought they perhaps would be. There's a lot more domestic violence than I was aware of. It's one of the things that struck me. (Social worker)

The focus of the team was on children and child protection. However, they had realized through using the tools that working with the adults in relation to domestic violence was also positive for the children. They had widened their perception of what constituted domestic violence and had better understanding of the dynamics involved. The social workers interviewed towards the end of the evaluation outlined the way their practice had shifted, as a result of using the tools, towards empowering women experiencing domestic violence. They found that empowerment came about, for instance, through naming the violence and identifying how it worked by reference to the Duluth power and control wheel, and that this gave back some control to the woman who had been abused:

because you're bringing it all out in the open, it almost seems to give them back a little bit of what they've lost… I suppose it is control of their lives. I suppose it is the power that their partner had over them. Because they are able to identify with what it is that's been going on, and also because they've got a name for it as well. (Social worker)

In some instances the tools had helped them in what otherwise appeared to be intractable situations. One senior social worker explained how in serious cases they had had good results:

> We complete an initial assessment and we manage to get the victims being empowered to actually make self-referrals to the Police Domestic Violence Unit, which a month or two before they were not going to be able to do it because they lacked the confidence. And that has happened a lot. (Senior social worker)

In one instance, where the domestic violence had been going on for a long time, the children were very disturbed as a result and two of them had been placed in residential care. The social worker attached to the case used the Duluth power and control wheel with the woman, and this was crucial to her making connections about what was happening to her and the children. She recognized that 'he does all of this'. She had since made drastic moves to change her parenting approach, was becoming redefined as a good parent and the social worker thought that the children would soon be returned to her care.

## Conclusion

This chapter has focused on the difficulties faced by social welfare agencies working with child protection issues in identifying domestic violence and working in supportive ways with mothers so that they are not held responsible or blamed for the abuse from their violent partners. The different traditions, theories and practice approaches regarding domestic violence, child protection, and visitation and contact create contradictions and lead to distinctions between violent men and men as fathers, making it easier to blame mothers for men's abuse towards them and their children. Yet, even where practitioners are concerned that their focus should be on the children and feel they do not understand what domestic violence is about, relatively simple solutions such as re-framing, screening, and use of the Duluth wheels may be used to change their practice, shifting it from mother blaming to a more positive and supportive approach.

10

# Conclusion – Linking the Three Planets

Writing this book has been a long process, evolving over some years from research into a number of facets of the 'three planets' (Hester 2004) we discussed in the previous chapter. Our ideas and our interest in this area of work are still very much 'work in progress' and it would be premature to offer conclusions in the conventional sense. We will, however, return to the issues we raised in the introductory chapter and hope that readers will draw on their own knowledge and expertise to take these ideas further.

## The impact of domestic violence on mothering

In writing this book, we have wanted to challenge mother blaming and re-focus attention from women's failures on to gender entrapment and how domestic violence perpetrators try to undermine women's relationships with children. Practitioners need to be aware of the complex and often hidden or 'normalized' ways in which domestic violence perpetrators actively continue their power and control over women and children. They need to consider the possibility of maltreatment and abuse to children where mothers are being abused and, vice versa, that mothers may be being abused where there is evidence of child maltreatment and abuse. Without asking about domestic violence, it may be unlikely that practitioners will know that domestic violence is an issue for the women and children concerned.

In drawing attention to the overlap between the perpetrator's domestic violence and his abuse and neglect of children, we do not claim that women who live with violent men are never neglectful or themselves abusive to their children. Research suggests that abused women are as likely as non-abused women to be violent or neglectful towards their children (Graham-Bermann and Edleson 2001). This is not, however, the only, nor necessarily the predominant, issue when assessing the child's safety in the context of domestic violence. Understanding how violent men may undermine women's parenting emotionally and materially may help professionals to respond more sensitively and build on women's own efforts to cope and be free from abuse, especially after separation. It is important to remember that violent men may use access to children to try to regain power and control over their ex-partners.

There needs to be a realistic appraisal that domestic violence is harmful to parenting, acknowledging women's own efforts to cope. Overcoming gender entrapment is a complex process in which women deal with domestic violence on a daily basis and often try to protect and shield children from abuse. These efforts can have contradictory consequences as the mother's efforts to shield a child and the child's efforts to protect the mother contribute to the conspiracy of silence about abuse. Training social workers, lawyers, shelter or refuge workers, CAFCASS (Children's Family Courts Advisory and Support Service) practitioners and health care professionals to talk to women frankly about domestic violence and mothering could provide many opportunities to move beyond the mother-blaming response, but this will be ineffective if steps are not also taken to try to stop the violence. It is also important that practitioners work with children to enhance their resilience and individual coping strategies.

## Re-framing the issues

We have tried to illustrate the complexity of gender entrapment in Hester's 'three planets' model where, whatever a woman does to protect her children in each of the three planets, her actions may be misconstrued as her failure to prioritize the children's interests. Clearly, there is a need to challenge the undermining of mothers in family law and social policy. This will include taking steps to eradicate battery by the law as we describe it in Chapter 6. Making safety a priority in assessment and case planning in domestic violence and abuse cases could help us to begin to address more adequately the mother's and the child's needs to have freedom from fear and peace at home. We have tried to stress the importance of assessing the specific needs of children in the context of their family relationships, taking into account how relationships may have been affected by the trauma associated with living with abuse. Research on child protection considered in the previous chapter points towards some positive findings from training health visitors and social workers in England to apply a domestic violence 'lens' when exploring a family's difficulties. If contact is to serve the interests of children, then there needs to be a willingness to challenge the dogmatic belief that contact with a biological parent must be preserved.

Although we have argued for safety to be a priority and for unhelpful beliefs such as the perceived contact presumption to be challenged, we would not support substituting one formulaic response to families living with domestic violence with another. One rigid belief we might propose is that assessments need to be relevant to the needs, risks, relationships and coping strategies/strengths in a particular family's circumstances.

## The need for further research

We have stressed the importance of taking into account how domestic violence impacts upon mothering when making assessments about a family's safety. The increased emphasis on risk assessment in recent years has brought a greater focus upon factors associated with high levels of risk for domestic violence. To further develop practice, experience gained in developing assessments (especially in family law and child protection) needs to be shared. In Chapter 8, we discussed a framework for assessment and argued that this should include an assessment of the possibility of trauma bonding between the violent parent and child. There is considerable scope to research and further develop the practice in making these assessments. In light of the difficulties presented by (scientifically suspect) assessments of parental alienation, false allegations and Munchausen Syndrome by Proxy, the need for developing an evidential basis for assessment is pressing.

In our discussion of violence and gender entrapment, we are aware that much more work needs to be done to explore further Beth Richie's (1995) pioneering research on how gender entrapment operates differently in the varied contexts of family, culture, ethnicity and social exclusion. The transnational nature of relationships and parenting raise additional risks and vulnerabilities for women and children, and additional issues for assessment and safe practice.

The attention given in crime reduction to evidence-based practice and evaluation research has only recently been turned towards 'what works' in family law and child protection (see, e.g. Trotter 2004). We do not know enough about what brings about change nor about which relationships change over time, for better or for worse. Although research discussed in this book indicates the importance of prioritizing safety when working with mothers living with domestic violence, further research is needed to investigate what factors might influence and sustain change over time. We do not know whether in the longer term safe contact services, parenting plans and perpetrator programmes contribute to better outcomes for women and children who have lived with domestic violence. It may be the case that some things work better for some individuals in some circumstances, but this is not the same for everybody. This is an important point to keep in mind and, if there is one main conclusion we would like you to draw from this book, it should be this: to understand the context of domestic violence, you need to explore this from the victim's and from the child's perspective.

## Mothering in the current context of public health and abuse

We have attempted to turn around mother blaming by showing how violent men use access to their own children as a route to abuse, to sustain power and control over mothers. Looking at domestic violence from a power and control perspective has highlighted emotional and psychological abuse and the harm caused to adult and child mental health. Increasingly, domestic and sexual violence are becoming recognized as widespread problems relevant to the broader public health agenda (McVeigh *et al.* 2005; Rose 2000). In the family courts and child protection, we have also observed a trend, in Europe at least, away from court-based litigation and legal 'solutions' to conflict towards harm-reduction, health-focused interventions. Recent proposals to amend family law and child protection in England have stressed the need to move away from risk-focused interventions and a pre-occupation with high-risk/high-conflict cases on to a more broadly based welfare-focused intervention (see DH 2003). The agreement focus of family law cases has been further developed into proposals to sift cases further out of the courts through case management that focuses on parenting plans that work from a welfare perspective with parents' difficulties and conflicts (see DCA 2004). In the past, efforts to boost the welfare focus of child protection or juvenile justice have brought perverse results of 'net widening', siphoning into the legal system more vulnerable families than previously was the case (Muncie 1998). There is the possibility that the public health agenda may help to marry the 'three planets' into a better multi-agency approach towards domestic violence. We need, though, to be mindful of the potential for the public health focus to create its own, new monsters on these planets.

# References

Abrahams, C. (1994) *The Hidden Victims – Children and Domestic Violence.* London: NCH Action for Children.

Advisory Board on Family Law (2000/2001) 'Making Contact Work'. A report to the Lord Chancellor on the facilitation of arrangements for contact between children and their non-residential parents and the enforcement of court orders for contact. February 2002. The Advisory Board on Family Law: Children Act Sub-Committee.

Armstrong, L. (2000) 'What happened when women said "Incest"'. In C. Itzin (ed.) *Home Truths About Child Sexual Abuse.* London: Routledge.

Ashworth, A. (1998) *Once in a House On Fire.* London: Picador.

Bala, N., Bertrand, L., Paetsch, J., Knoppers, B., Hornick, J., Noel, J., Boudreau, L. and Miklas, S. (1998) *Spousal Violence in Custody and Access Disputes: Recommendations for Reform.* Ottowa, Canada: Status of Women in Canada.

Blum, D. (1998) 'Finding Strength: How to Overcome Everything'. *Psychology Today,* May-June.

Bowker, L., Arbitell, M. and McFerron, J. (1988) 'On the Relationship Between Wife Beating and Child Abuse'. In K. Yllo and M. Bograd (eds) *Feminist Perspectives on Wife Abuse.* London: Sage.

Bowlby, J. (1982) *Attachment and Loss: Volume 1: Attachment.* New York: Basic Books.

Brandon, M. and Lewis, A. (1996) 'Significant Harm and Children's Experiences of Domestic Violence'. *Child and Family Social Work 1,* 1, 33–42.

Bream, V. and Buchanan, A. (2003) 'Distress among children whose separated or divorced parents cannot agree arrangements for them'. *British Journal of Social Work 33,* 227–238.

Bridge Child Care Consultancy (1991) *Sukina: An Evaluation of the Circumstances Leading to Her Death.* London: Bridge Child Care Consultancy Service.

British Medical Association (1998) *Domestic Violence. A Healthcare Issue?* London: British Medical Association.

Bullock, L. and McFarlane, J. (1989) 'The Birth Weight/Battering Connection'. *American Journal of Nursing 89,* 1153–1155.

Burton, S., Regan, L. and Kelly, L. (1998) *Supporting Women and Challenging Men: Lessons from the Domestic Violence Intervention Project.* Bristol: Policy Press.

Busch, R. (1998) 'Domestic Violence, Custody and Access in New Zealand'. Paper presented to 4th International Conference on Children Exposed to Family Violence. London Ontario.

Campbell, J. (1998) 'Making the Health Care System an Empowerment Zone for Battered Women'. In J. Campbell (ed.) *Empowering Survivors of Abuse: Health Care for Battered Women and Their Children.* Thousand Oaks, CA: Sage.

Campbell, J., Oliver, C. and Bullock, L. (1998a) 'The Dynamics of Battering During Pregnancy: Women's Explanations of Why'. In J. Campbell (ed.) *Empowering Survivors of Abuse: Health Care for Battered Women and Their Children.* Thousand Oaks, CA: Sage.

Campbell, J., Soeken, K., McFarlane, J. and Parker, B. (1998b) 'Risk Factors for Femicide amongst Pregnant and Non-Pregnant Battered Women'. In J. Campbell (ed.) *Empowering Survivors of Abuse.* Thousand Oaks, CA and London: Sage.

Cantwell, B. and Nunnerley, M. (1996) 'A new spotlight on family mediation'. *Family Law 26,* 177–180.

Cawson, P. (2002) *Child Maltreatment in the Family: The experiences of a National Sample of Young People.* London: NSPCC.

Chetwin, A., Knaggs, T., Te Wairere Ahiahi and Young, P. (1999) *The Domestic Violence Legislation and Child Access in New Zealand.* Wellington: Ministry of Justice.

Children Act Sub-Committee (2000) *A Report to the Lord Chancellor on the Question of Parental Contact in Cases where there is Domestic Violence.* London: Lord Chancellor's Department.

Cleaver, H. and Freeman, P. (1995) *Parental Perspectives in Cases of Suspected Child Abuse.* London: HMSO.

Cleaver, H. Unell, I. and Aldgate, J. (1999) *Children's Needs – Parenting Capacity: The Impact of Parental Mental Illness, Problem Alcohol and Drug Use, and Domestic Violence on Children's Development.* London: HMSO.

Conte, J. (1992) 'Has this Child been Sexually Abused?' *Criminal Justice and Behaviour 19,* 1, 54.

Cook, D., Burton, M., Robinson, A. and Vallely, C. (2004) *Evaluation of Specialist Domestic Violence Courts/Fast Track Systems.* London: CPS/DCA/Criminal Justice Race Unit.

Corvo, K. and Johnson, P. (2003) 'Villification of the Batterer – How Blame Shapes Domestic Violence Policy and Intervention'. *Aggression and Violent Behaviour 8,* 3, May–June, 259–281.

Cummings, E. M., Zahn-Waxler, C. and Radke-Yarrow, M. (1984) 'Developmental Changes in Children's Reactions to Anger in the Home'. *Child Psychology and Child Psychiatry 25,* 63–74.

Daly, M. and Wilson, M. (1988) *Homicide.* Hawthorne, NY: Aldine de Gruyter.

Davis, L.V. and Carlson, B.E. (1987) 'Observations of Spouse Abuse. What Happens to the Children?' *Journal of Interpersonal Violence 2,* 3, 278–291.

Debbonnaire, T. (1994) 'Work with Women in Women's Aid Refuges and After'. In A. Mullender and R. Morley (eds) *Children Living with Domestic Violence.* London: Whiting and Birch.

DCA (Department of Constitutional Affairs) (2004) *Consultation Paper on Parental Separation.* London: DCA.

DH (Department of Health) (1995) *Messages from Research.* London: HMSO.

DH (1997a) *The Children Act – Guidance and Regulations.* London: DH.

DH (1997b) Local Authority Circular LAC(97) 15, *Family Law Act 1996. Part IV Family Homes and Domestic Violence.* London: DH.

DH (1999) *Working Together to Safeguard Children.* London: DH.

DH (2003) *Every Child Matters.* London: DH.

DH (2005) *Domestic Abuse Manual for Health Care Professionals.* London: DH, available online from www.doh.gov.uk

Dobash, R. and Dobash, R.E. (1980) *Violence Against Wives.* Sussex: Open Books.

Dobash, R.E. and Dobash, R.P. (1984) 'The Nature and Antecedent of Violent Events'. *British Journal of Criminology 24,* 3, 269–288.

Dobash, R. and Dobash, R. (1992) *Women, Violence and Social Change.* London: Routledge.

Dobash, R. E. and Dobash, R. (1998) 'Violent Men and Violent Contexts'. In R. Dobash and R. Dobash (eds) *Re-thinking Violence against Women.* London: Sage.

Dominy, N. and Radford, L. (1996) *Domestic Violence in Surrey: Towards an Effective Inter-agency Response.* Surrey County Council Social Services/University of Surrey, Roehampton.

Douglas, A. (2005) Speech delivered at launch of Stephen's Place, Hammersmith and Fulham Domestic Violence Intervention Programme, Children's Service Safe Contact Centre, March.

Doyne, S., Bowermaster, J., Reid Meloy, J., Dutton, D., Jaffe, P., Temko, S. and Mones, P. (1999) 'Custody Disputes Involving Domestic Violence: Making Children's Needs a Priority'. *Juvenile and Family Court Journal,* spring, 1–12.

Edleson, J.L. (1995) 'Mothers and Children: Understanding the Links between Woman Battering and Child Abuse'. Paper presented at the Strategic Planning Workshop on Violence against Women. Washington: National Institute of Justice.

Edleson, J. L. (1999) 'Children's Witnessing of Adult Domestic Violence'. *Journal of Interpersonal Violence 8,* 14, 839–871.

Edleson, J. L. (2001) 'Studying the Co-occurrence of Child Maltreatment and Domestic Violence in Families'. In S. Graham-Bermann and J. Edleson (eds) *Domestic Violence in the Lives of Children: The*

*Future of Research, Intervention and Social Policy.* Washington, DC: American Psychological Association, pp.91–110.

Edleson, J. L. and Tolman, R. (1992) *Intervention for Men who Batter.* London: Sage.

Edleson, J. L., Daro, D. and Pinderhughes, H. (2004) 'Finding a Common Agenda for Preventing Child Maltreatment, Youth Violence, and Domestic Violence'. *Journal of Interpersonal Violence 19*, 3, 279–281.

Edleson, J. L., Mbilinyi, L. F., Beeman, S. K. and Hagemeister, A. K. (2003) 'How Children are Involved in Adult Domestic Violence'. *Journal of Interpersonal Violence 18*, 1, 18–32.

Epstein, C. and Keep, G. (1995) 'What Children tell Childline about Domestic Violence'. In A. Saunders with C. Epstein, G. Keep and T. Debbonaire (eds) *It Hurts Me Too: Children's Experiences of Domestic Violence and Refuge Life.* Bristol: WAFE/Childline/NISW.

Eriksson, M. and Hester, M. (2001) 'Violent Men as Good-Enough Fathers? A Look at England and Sweden'. *Violence Against Women 7*, 7, 779–798.

ESRC Violence Research Programme (1998) *Taking Stock: What do we Know about Violence?* ESRC Violence Research Programme: Brunel University, Uxbridge.

Everitt, A., Hardiker, P., Littlewood, J. and Mullender, A. (1992) *Applied Research for Better Practice.* Basingstoke: Macmillan.

Families Need Fathers (1993) 'Memorandum 13', *Home Affairs Committee Third Report: Domestic Violence, Volume II*, Cm 245-II. London: HMSO.

Farmer, E. and Owen, M. (1995) *Child Protection Practice: Private Risks and Public Remedies.* London: HMSO.

Farmer, E. and Pollock, S. (1998) *Substitute Care for Sexually Abused and Abusing Children.* Chichester: Wiley.

Fineman, M. (1989) 'The Politics of Custody and Gender: Child Advocacy and the Transformation of Custody Decision Making in the USA'. In C. Smart and S. Sevenhuijsen (eds) *Child Custody and The Politics of Gender.* London: Routledge.

Forman, J. (1995) *Is there a Correlation between Child Sexual Abuse and Domestic Violence? An Exploratory Study of the Links between Child Sexual Abuse and Domestic Violence in a Sample of Intrafamilial Child Sexual Abuse Cases.* Glasgow: Women's Support Project.

Fuszara, M. (1997) 'The activities of family courts in Poland'. *International Journal of Law, Policy and the Family 11*, 1, 86–102.

Gardner, R. (1985) 'Recent Trends in Divorce and Custody Litigation'. *Academy Forum 29*, 2, 13–17.

Garland, D. (2001) *The Culture of Control: Crime and Social Order in Contemporary Society.* Oxford: Oxford University Press.

Garmezy, N. and Rutter, M. (1988) (eds) *Stress, Coping and Development in Children.* New York: McGraw Hill.

Garrity, C. and Baris, M. (1995) 'Custody and Visitation: Is it Safe?' *Family Advocate 17*, 3, Winter, 40–45.

Gelles, R. (1988) 'Violence and Pregnancy: Are Pregnant Women at Greater Risk of Abuse?' *Journal of Marriage and the Family 50*, 841–847.

Gibbons, J., Conroy, S. and Bell, C. (1995) *Operating the Child Protection System: A Study of Child Protection Practices in English Local Authorities.* London: HMSO.

Gilchrist, E., Johnson, R., Takriti, R., Weston, S., Beech, A. and Kebbell, M. (2003) *Domestic Violence Offenders: Characteristics and Offending Related Needs: Findings No 217*, Home Office Research, Development and Statistics Directorate, London.

Gill, A. and Sharma, K. (2005) 'No Access to Justice: Gender, Violence and Immigration Law'. *Safe,* Autumn, 15–18.

Glass, D. (1995) *All my Fault: Why Women don't Leave Abusive Men.* London: Virago.

Golding, J. (1999) 'Intimate Partner Abuse as a Risk Factor for Mental Disorder: a Meta-analysis.' *Journal of Family Violence 14*, 2, 99–132.

Gould, J. (1998) *Conducting Scientifically Crafted Child Custody Evaluations.* London: Sage.

Graham-Bermann, S. and Edleson, J. (2001) (eds) *Domestic Violence in the Lives of Children: The Future of Research, Intervention and Social Policy.* Washington: American Psychological Association.

Grillo, T. (1991) 'The Mediation Alternative: Process Dangers for Women'. *Yale Law Journal 100*, 1545–1610.

Grusznski, R.J., Brink, J.C. and Edleson, J.L. (1988) 'Support and Education Groups for Children of Battered Women'. *Child Welfare 67*, 5, 431–444.

Hague, G. and Malos, E. (1996) *Tackling Domestic Violence: A Guide to Developing Multi-Agency Initiatives.* Bristol: Policy Press.

Hague, G. M., Mullender, A. and Aris, R. (2004) 'Listening to Women's Voices: the Participation of Domestic Violence Survivors in Services'. In T. Skinner, M. Hester and E. Malos (eds) *Researching Gender Violence: Feminist Methodology in Action.* Devon: Willan Publishing.

Hague, G., Mullender, A., Kelly, L. and Malos, E. (2000) 'Unsung Innovation: the History of Work with Children in UK Domestic Violence Refuges'. In J. Hanmer and C. Itzin (eds) *Home Truths about Domestic Violence. Feminist Influences on Policy and Practice.* London and New York: Routledge.

Hague, G., Kelly, L., Malos, E., Mullender, A. with Debbonaire, T. (1996) *Children, Domestic Violence and Refuges: A Study of Needs and Responses.* Bristol: Women's Aid Federation (England).

Hampton, R., Jenkins, P. and Vandergriff-Amery, M. (1999) 'Physical and Sexual Violence in Marriage'. In R. Hampton (ed.) *Family Violence: Prevention and Treatment,* 2nd edn. Thousand Oaks, CA: Sage.

Harne, L. (2004) 'Childcare, Violence and Fathering – Are Violent Fathers who Look After their Children Likely to be Less Abusive?' In R. Klein and B. Wallner (eds) *Gender, Conflict and Violence,* Vienna: Studien-Verlag.

Harris Hendriks, J., Black, D. and Kaplan, T. (1993) *When Father Kills Mother. Guiding Children Through Trauma and Grief.* London: Routledge.

Haynes, J. (1990) *The Fundamentals of Family Mediation.* London: Old Bailey Press.

Hearn, J. (1996) 'Men's Violence to Known Women: Historical and Theoretical Constructions'. In B. Featherstone, J. Hearn, and C. Toft (eds) *Violence and Gender Relations: Theories and Interventions.* London: Sage, pp.23–37.

Hearn, J. (1998) *The Violences of Men.* London: Sage.

Heiskanen, M. and Piispa, M. (1998) *Faith, Hope and Battering: A Survey of Men's Violence against Women.* Helsinki: Statistics Finland.

HMIC/HMCPSI (2004) *Her Majesty's Inspectorate of Constabulary and Her Majesty's Council for Probation Service Inspectorate Report on Violence at Home,* available online from www.hmcpsi.gov.uk/reports/DomViol0104Rep.pdf

HMICA (2005) *Domestic Violence, Safety and Family Proceedings: Thematic Review of the Handling of Domestic Violence Issues by the Children's Family Courts Advisory and Support Service (CAFCASS) and the Administration of Family Courts in Her Majesty's Courts Service (HMCS)* London: Her Majesty's Inspectorate of Court Administration, available online from www.hmica.gov.uk

Herman, J. (2001) *Trauma and Recovery: From Domestic Abuse to Political Terror.* London: Pandora.

Hershorn, M. and Rosenbaum, A. (1985) 'Children of Marital Violence: A closer look at unintended victims'. *American Journal of Orthopsychiatry 55,* 260–266.

Hester, M. (2000) 'Child Protection and Domestic Violence: Findings from a Rowntree/NSPCC Study'. In C. Itzin, J. Hanmer, S. Quaid and D. Wigglesworth (eds) *Home Truths About Domestic Violence.* London: Routledge.

Hester, M. (2002) 'One Step Forward and Three Steps Back? Children, Abuse and Parental Contact in Denmark'. *Child and Family Law Quarterly 14,* 3, 267–279.

Hester, M. (2004) 'Future Trends and Developments – Violence against Women in Europe and East Asia'. *Violence Against Women 10,* 12.

Hester M. (2005) 'Children, Abuse and Parental Contact in Denmark'. In M. Eriksson, M. Hester, S. Keskinen and K. Pringle (eds) *Tackling Men's Violence in Families – Nordic Issues and Dilemmas.* Bristol: Policy Press.

Hester, M. (2006) 'Asking About Domestic Violence – Implications for Practice'. In C. Humphreys and N. Stanley *Domestic Violence and Child Protection.* London: Jessica Kingsley Publishers.

Hester, M. and Harne, L. (1999) 'Fatherhood, Children and Violence – The UK in an International Perspective'. In S. Watson and L. Doyal, L (eds) *Engendering Social Policy.* Milton Keynes: Open University Press.

Hester, M. and Pearson, C. (1998) *From Periphery to Centre: Domestic Violence in Work with Abused Children.* Bristol: Policy Press, published 2000 by Jessica Kingsley Publishers.

Hester, M. and Radford, L. (1992) 'Domestic Violence and Access Arrangements for Children in Denmark and Britain'. *Journal of Social Welfare and Family Law 1*, 57–70.

Hester, M. and Radford, L. (1996a) *Domestic Violence and Child Contact Arrangements in England and Denmark.* Bristol: Policy Press.

Hester, M. and Radford, L. (1996b) 'Contradictions and Compromises: The Impact of The Children Act 1989 on Women and Children's Safety'. In M. Hester, L. Kelly and J. Radford (eds) *Women, Violence and Male Power.* Milton Keynes: Open University Press, pp.81–98.

Hester, M. and Scott, J. (2000) *Women in Abusive Relationships: Group Work and Agency Support.* London: Barnados.

Hester, M. and Westmarland, N. (2005) *Tackling Domestic Violence: Effective Interventions and Approaches.* Home Office Research Study 290. London: Home Office.

Hester, M. Pearson, C. and Radford, L. (1997) *Domestic Violence: A National Survey of Court Welfare and Voluntary Sector Mediation Practice.* Bristol: Policy Press.

Hester, M., Pearson, C. and Harwin, N. with Abrahams, H. (2006) *Making an Impact – Children and Domestic Violence.* 2nd edn. London: Jessica Kingsley Publishers.

Hilton, N.Z. (1992) 'Battered Women's Concerns about their Children Witnessing Wife Assault'. *Journal of Interpersonal Violence 7, 1,* 77–86.

Hoff, L. (1990) *Battered Women as Survivors.* London: Routledge.

Holden, G. and Ritchie, K. (1991) 'Linking Extreme Marital Discord, Child Rearing and Child Behaviour Problems: Evidence from Battered Women'. *Child Development 62,* 311–332.

Holden, G., Stein, J., Ritchie, K., Harris, S. and Jouniles, E. (1998) 'Parenting Behaviours and Beliefs of Battered Women'. In G. Holden, R. Geffner and E. Jouniles (eds) *Children Exposed To Marital Violence: Theory, Research and Applied Issues.* Washington, DC: American Psychological Association.

Home Office (1999) *Criminal Statistics.* London: Home Office.

Home Office (2000) *Home Office Circular 19/2000; Domestic Violence.* London: Home Office.

Hooper, C. (1992) *Mothers of Sexually Abused Children.* London: Routledge.

Hooper, C. (1995) 'Women's and their Children's Experiences of Domestic Violence: Rethinking the Links'. *Women's Studies International Forum 18,* 3, 349–360.

Horley, S. (2002) *Power and Control; Why Charming Men Can Make Dangerous Lovers.* Basingstoke: Papermac.

Hudson, R. (1996) 'Contact and Domestic Violence'. *NLJ Practitioner,* October: 1549.

Hughes, H.M. (1988) 'Psychological and Behavioural Correlates of Family Violence in Child Witnesses and Victims'. *American Journal of Orthopsychiatry 58,* 1, 77–90.

Hughes, H. (1992) 'Impact of Spouse Abuse on Children of Battered Women'. *Violence Update 1,* 9–11.

Hughes, H., Graham-Bermann, S. and Gruber, G. (2001) 'Resilience in Children Exposed to Domestic Violence'. In S. Graham-Bermann and J. Edleson (eds) *Domestic Violence in the Lives of Children: The Future of Research, Intervention and Social Policy.* Washington: American Psychological Association, pp.67–90.

Hughes, H.M., Parkinson, D. and Vargo, M. (1989) 'Witnessing spouse abuse and experiencing physical abuse: a "double whammy"?' *Journal of Family Violence 4,* 2, 197–209.

Humphreys, C. (1997) 'Child Sexual Abuse: Allegations in the Context of Divorce: Issues for Mothers'. *British Journal of Social Work 27,* 529–44.

Humphreys, C. (2000) *Social Work, Domestic Violence and Child Protection: Challenging Practice.* Bristol: Policy Press.

Humphreys, C. (2006) 'Relevant Evidence for Practice'. In C. Humphreys and N. Stanley (eds) *Domestic Violence and Child Protection.* London: Jessica Kingsley Publishers.

Humphreys, C. and Thiara, R. (2003) 'Mental Health and Domestic Violence: I call it symptoms of abuse'. *British Journal of Social Work 33,* 209–226.

Humphreys, C., Hester, M., Hague, G., Mullender, A., Abrahams, H. and Lowe, P. (2000) *From Good Intentions to Good Practice – Mapping Services for Families where there is Domestic Violence.* Bristol: Policy Press, in association with Joseph Rowntree Foundation.

Humphreys, C. and Harrison, C. (2003) 'Focusing on Safety: Domestic Violence and the Role of Child Contact Centres'. *Child and Family Law Quarterly 15,* 3, 237–253.

Hunt, J. and Roberts, C. (2004) *Child Contact with Non-Resident Parents.* Family Policy Briefing 3, January, Oxford: Department of Social Policy and Social Work, University of Oxford.

Jackson, S., Feder, L., Forde, D., Davis, R., Maxwell, C. and Taylor, B. (2003) *Batterer Intervention Programmes: Where Do We Go From Here?* Washington: National Institute of Justice.

Jaffe, P., Wolfe, D. and Wilson, S. (1990) *Children of Battered Women.* Thousand Oaks, California: Sage.

Jaffe, P., Poisson, S. and Cunningham, A. (2001) 'Domestic Violence and High Conflict Divorce: Developing a New Generation of Research for Children'. In S. Graham-Bermann and J. Edleson, (eds) *Domestic Violence in the Lives of Children: The Future of Research, Intervention and Social Policy.* Washington: American Psychological Association, pp.189–202.

Jaffe, P., Lemon, N. and Poisson, S. (2003) *Child Custody and Domestic Violence: A Call For Safety and Accountability.* Thousand Oaks, California: Sage.

James, G. (1994) *Study of Working Together Part 8 Reports,* London: Department of Health.

James-Hanmen, D. (2000) 'Enhancing Multi-Agency Work'. In J. Hanmer and C. Itzin (eds) *Home Truths about Domestic Violence.* London: Routledge.

Johnson, H. (1998) 'Rethinking Survey Research on Violence against Women'. In R. E. Dobash and R. P. Dobash (eds) *Rethinking Violence against Women.* Thousand Oaks, London, New Delhi: Sage, pp.23–51.

Johnston, J. (1993) 'Gender, Violent Conflict and Mediation'. *Family Mediation 3,* 2, 9–13.

Jouriles, E. N., Barling, J. and O'Leary, K. D. (1987) 'Predicting Child Behaviour Problems in Martially Violent Families'. *Journal of Abnormal Child Psychology 15,* 165–173.

Kashani, J. and Allan, W. (1998) *The Impact of Family Violence on Children and Adolescents.* London: Sage.

Kaye, M., Stubbs, J. and Tolmie, J. (2003) *Negotiating Child Residence and Contact Arrangements against a Background of Domestic Violence.* Research Report 1, June, Socio-Legal Research Centre, Natham: Griffiths University.

Kelly, L. (1988) *Surviving Sexual Violence.* Oxford: Polity.

Kelly, L. (1996) 'When Woman Protection is the Best Kind of Child Protection: Children, Domestic Violence and Child Abuse'. *Administration 44,* 2, 118–135.

Kelly, L., Regan, L. and Burton, S. (1991) *An Exploratory Study of the Prevalence of Sexual Abuse in a Sample of 1200 16 to 21 Year Olds.* Final report to the ESRC. London: Child Abuse Studies Unit, University of North London.

Kemshall, H. (1996) *Reviewing Risk: A Review of the Research on the Assessment and Management of Risk and Dangerousness: Implications for Policy and Practice in the Probation Service.* Home Office Research and Statistics Directorate, London: Home Office.

Kemshall, H. (2002) *Understanding Risk in Criminal Justice.* Maidenhead, Buckingham: Open University Press.

Kolbo, J., Blakely, E.H. and Engleman, D. (1996) 'Children who Witness Domestic Violence: A Review of Empirical Literature'. *Journal of Interpersonal Violence 11,* 2, 281–293.

Kropp, P., Hart, S., Webster, C. and Eaves, D. (1999) *The Spousal Assault Risk Assessment (SARA) Guide User's Manual.* Toronto, Canada: Multi-Health Systems Inc. and B.C. Institute Against Family Violence.

Lees, S. (1997) *Ruling Passions.* London: Routledge.

Lemon, N. (1996) *Domestic Violence Law: A Comprehensive Overview of Cases and Sources.* Austin and Winfield: San Francisco.

Levine, M.B. (1975) 'Interparental Violence and its Effect on the Children: A Study of 50 Families in General Practice'. *Medicine, Science and the Law 15,* 3, 172–176.

Liss, M. and Stahly, G. (1993) 'Domestic Violence and Child Custody'. In M. Hansen and M. Harway (eds) *Battering and Family Therapy: A Feminist Perspective.* Newbury Park, CA: Sage.

London Borough of Greenwich (1987) *A Child in Mind: Protection of Children in a Responsible Society. Report of the Commission of Inquiry into the Circumstances Surrounding the Death of Kimberley Carlile.* London: London Borough of Greenwich.

Lundgren, E., Heimer, G., Westerstrand, J. and Kalliokoski, A-M. (2001) *Slagen dam* [Captured Queen]. Stockholm and Umeå: Fritzes and Brottsoffermyndigheten.

Maccoby, E. and Mnookin, R. (1992) *Dividing the Child: Social and Legal Dilemmas of Custody.* Cambridge, MA: Harvard University Press.

Malos, E. and Hague, G. (1993) 'Homelessness and Domestic Violence: The Effect on Children and Young People'. *Childright 99,* 15–19.

Mason, M. (1999) *The Custody Wars: Why Children are Losing the Legal Battle and What We Can Do About It.* New York: Basic Books.

Maynard, M. (1985) 'The Response of Social Workers to Domestic Violence'. In J. Pahl (ed.) *Private Violence and Public Policy.* London: Routledge.

McGee, C. (1996) 'Children's and Mothers' Experiences of Child Protection Following Domestic Violence'. Paper given at *Violence, Abuse and Women's Citizenship International Conference,* Brighton.

McGee, C. (2000) *Childhood Experiences of Domestic Violence.* London: Jessica Kingsley Publishers.

McMahon, M., Neville-Sorvilles, J. and Schubert, L. (1999) 'Undoing Harm to Children: The Duluth Family Visitation Center'. In M. Shepard and E. Pence (eds) *Coordinating Community Responses to Domestic Violence: Lessons From Duluth and Beyond.* London: Sage.

McVeigh, C., Hughes, K., Bellis, M., Ashton, J. and Syed, Q. (2005) *Violent Britain: People, Prevention and Public Health.* WHO/Centre for Public Health, Liverpool: John Moores University.

McWilliams, M. and McKiernan, J. (1993) *Bringing It Out in the Open: Domestic Violence in Northern Ireland.* Belfast: HMSO.

Mertin, P. (1995) 'A Follow Up Study of Children from Domestic Violence'. *Australian Journal of Family Law 9,* 76–85.

Mezey, G.C. and Bewley, S. (1997) 'Domestic violence and pregnancy'. *British Medical Journal 314.*

Mirlees-Black, C. (1999) *Domestic Violence: Findings from a New British Crime Survey Self-Completion Questionnaire.* London: Home Office.

Mirlees-Black, C., Budd, T., Partridge, S. and Mayhew, P. (1998) *The 1998 British Crime Survey.* London: Home Office.

Moore, T., Pepler, D., Weinberg, B., Hammond, L., Waddell, J. and Weiser, L. (1990) 'Research on Children from Violent Families'. *Canada's Mental Health,* 19–23.

Morrow, M., Hankivsky, O. and Varcoe, C. (2004) 'Women and Violence: The Effects of Dismantling the Welfare State'. *Critical Social Policy 24,* 3, 358–384.

Mullender, A. (1996) *Re-Thinking Domestic Violence: The Social Work and Probation Response.* London: Routledge.

Mullender, A., Hague, G., Iman, U., Kelly, L., Malos, E. and Regan, L. (2002) *Children's Perspectives on Domestic Violence.* London: Sage.

Mullender, A., Burton, S., Hague, G., Imam, U., Kelly, L., Malos, E. and Regan, L. (2003) '*Stop Hitting Mum!' Children Talk About Domestic Violence.* Sussex: Young Voice.

Muncie, J. (1998) 'Give 'Em What They Deserve: The Young Offender and Youth Justice Policy'. In M. Langan (ed.) *Welfare Needs, Rights and Risks.* London: Routledge, pp.171–214.

Murray, K. (1999) 'When Children Refuse to Visit Parents: Is Prison an Appropriate Remedy?' *Family and Conciliation Courts Review 37,* 1, January, 83–98.

National Children's Bureau (1993) *Investigation into Inter-Agency Practice following the Cleveland Area Child Protection Committee's Report Concerning the Death of Toni Dales.* London: National Children's Bureau.

National Council of Juvenile and Family Court Judges (1994) 'Model Code on Domestic and Family Violence,' available online from www.ncjfc.org/images/stories/dept/fvd/pdf/new_modelcode.pdf. Accessed June 2006.

Nichols, L. and Feltey, K. (2003) '"The Woman is not Always the Bad Guy": Dominant Discourse and Resistance in the Lives of Battered Women'. *Violence Against Women 9,* 7, July, 784–806.

Oakley, A. (1980) *Becoming a Mother.* Martin Robinson: Oxford.

O'Hara, M. (1994) 'Child Deaths in the Context of Domestic Violence: Implications for Professional Practice'. In A. Mullender and R. Morley (eds) *Children Living with Domestic Violence: Putting Men's Abuse of Women on the Child Care Agenda*. London: Whiting and Birch.

O'Quigley, A. (2000) *Listening to Children's Views: The Findings and Recommendations of Recent Research*. York: Joseph Rowntree Foundation.

O'Sullivan, C. (2000) 'Estimating the Population at Risk for Violence during Child Visitation'. *Domestic Violence Report 5*, 77–79.

Pahl, J. (1985) *Private Violence and Public Policy*. London: Routledge.

Parton, N. (1990) *The Politics of Child Abuse*. London: RKP.

Peled, E. and Davis, D. (1995) *Groupwork with Children of Battered Women: A Practitioner's Manual*. Thousand Oaks, CA: Sage.

Radford, L. (2000) 'Domestic Violence'. In M. May, E. Brunsden and R. Page (eds) *Social Problems*. London: Macmillan.

Radford, L. (2004a) 'Programmed or Licensed to Kill? The New Biology of Femicide'. In D. Rees and S. Rose (eds) *The New Brain Sciences: Perils and Prospects*. Cambridge: Cambridge University Press, pp.131–148.

Radford, L. (2004b) 'Peace at Home – Safety and Parental Contact Arrangements for Children in the Context of Domestic Violence'. In C. Breen (ed.) *Children's Needs, Rights and Welfare: Developing Strategies for the 'Whole Child' in the 21st Century*. Palmerston North: Thomson Dunmore Press, pp.85–104.

Radford, L. and Cappel, C. (2003) *The Way Forward: Domestic Violence and the Methodist Church*. Research Report to Methodist Church Women's Network UK, London.

Radford, L. and Gill, A. (2004) *Moving Forward on Prevention: Domestic Violence and Community Safety in West Sussex*. London: University of Surrey.

Radford, L., Blacklock, N. and Iwi, K. (2006) 'Domestic Risk Assessment and Safety Planning in Child Protection – Assessing Perpetrators'. In C. Humphreys and N. Stanley (eds) *Social Work and Child Protection*. London: Jessica Kingsley Publishers.

Radford, L., Sayer, S. and AMICA (1999) *Unreasonable Fears: Child Contact in the Context of Domestic Violence: A Survey of Mothers' Perceptions of Harm*. Bristol: Women's Aid Federation.

Rhodes, H., Graycar, R. and Harrison, M. (1999) *The Family Law Reform Act: Can Changing Legislation Change Legal Culture, Legal Practice and Community Expectations?* Interim Report, Family Court of Australia/University of Sydney, Faculty of Law.

Richie, B. (1995) *Compelled to Crime: The Gender Entrapment of Black Battered Women*. London: Routledge.

Roberts, G., Hegarty, G. and Feder, G. (2005) (eds) *Intimate Partner Abuse and Health Professionals: Old Problems, New Approaches to Domestic Violence*. Oxford: Elsevier Churchill Livingstone.

Roberts, M. (1994) 'Who is in charge? Effecting a productive exchange between researchers and practitioners in the field of family mediation'. *Journal of Social Welfare and Family Law 4*, 439–454.

Rodgers, B. and Pryor, J. (1998) *Divorce and Separation: The Outcomes for Children*. York: Joseph Rowntree Foundation.

Rose, N. (2000) 'Government and Control'. *British Journal of Criminology 40*, Special Issue on Criminology and Social Theory, 321–399.

Ross, S.M. (1996) 'Risk of Physical Abuse to Children of Spouse Abusing Parents'. *Child Abuse and Neglect 20*, 7, 589–598.

Rossman, B. and Rosenberg, M. (1992) 'Family Stress in Children; The Moderating Effects of Children's Beliefs about their Control over Parental Conflict'. *Journal of Clinical Psychology and Psychiatry 33*, 699–715.

Rossman, R. (2001) 'Longer Term Effects of Children's Exposure to Domestic Violence'. In S. Graham-Burmann and J. Edleson (eds) *Domestic Violence in the Lives of Children: The Future of Research, Intervention and Social Policy*. Washington, D. American Psychological Association.

Russell, D. (1982) *Rape in Marriage*. Bloomington: Indiana University Press.

Rutter, M. (1985) 'Resilience in the Face of Adversity: Protective Factors and Resistance to Psychiatric Disorders'. *British Journal of Psychiatry 147*, 598–611.

Rutter, M. (1988) 'Stress, Coping and Development'. In N. Garmezy and M. Rutter (eds) *Stress, Coping and Development in Children*. Baltimore: John Hopkins University Press, pp.1–42.

Saunders, A. with Epstein, C., Keep, G. and Debbonaire, T. (1995) *It Hurts Me Too: Children's Experiences of Domestic Violence and Refuge Life*. Bristol: WAFE/Childline/NISW.

Saunders, H. (2001) Speech by Hilary Saunders, National Children's Officer, Women's Aid Federation of England.

Saunders, H. and Barron, J. (2003) *Failure to Protect*. Bristol: Women's Aid Federation England.

Schecter, S. and Edleson, J. (1999) *The Green Book: Effective Intervention in Woman Battering and Child Maltreatment Cases: Guidelines for Policy and Practice: Recommendations from the National Council of Juvenile and Family Court Judges Family Violence Department*. Nevada: National Council of Juvenile and Family Court Judges.

Schornstein, S. (1997) *Domestic Violence and Health Care*. Thousand Oaks, CA: Sage.

Sinclair, R. and Bullock, R. (2002) *Learning From Past Experience: A Review of Serious Case Reviews*. DH, June.

Smart, C. and Sevenhuisen, S. (1989) *Child Custody and the Politics of Gender*. London: Routledge.

Smart, C., Neale, B. and Wade, A. (2001) *The Changing Experience of Childhood: Families and Divorce*. Oxford: Polity.

Soothill, K., Francis, B., Ackerley, E., Fligelstone, R. and Ranelli, G. (2002) *Murder and Serious Sexual Assault*. Police Research Series Paper 144. London: Home Office.

Stanko, E., Crisp, D., Hale, C. and Lucraft, H. (1998) *Counting the Costs: Estimating the Impact of Domestic Violence in the London Borough of Hackney*. London: Crime Concern.

Stark, E. and Flitcraft, A.H. (1988) 'Women and Children at Risk: A Feminist Perspective on Child Abuse'. *International Journal of Health Studies 18*, 1, 97–119.

Stark, E. and Flitcraft, A. (1996) *Women at Risk: Domestic Violence and Women's Health*. Thousand Oaks, CA: Sage.

Stark, E., Flitcraft, A. and Frazier, W. (1979) 'Medicine and Patriarchal Violence; The Social Construction of a Private Event'. *International Journal of Health Services 9*, 461–493.

Strategic Partners Pty Ltd (1998) *Contact Services in Australia: Research and Evaluation Project Final Report*. Online at www.facs.gov.au/internet/facsinternet.nsf/family/frsp-ccs_ research.htm. Accessed June 2006.

Sturge, C. and Glaser, D. (2000) 'Contact and Domestic Violence – The Experts' Court Report'. *Family Law*, September, 615–629.

Sullivan, C. M. and Bybee, D. I. (1999) 'Reducing Violence Using Community Based Advocacy for Women with Abusive Partners'. *Journal of Consulting and Clinical Psychology 67*, 1, 43–53.

Taylor-Browne, J. (2001) *What Works in Reducing Domestic Violence?* London: Whiting and Birch.

Thoburn, J., Lewis, A. and Shemmings, D. (1995) *Paternalism or Partnership? Family Involvement in the Child Protection Process*. London: HMSO.

Thoennes, N. and Tjaden, P. (1991) 'The Extent, Nature and Validity of Sexual Abuse Allegations in Custody/Visitation Disputes'. *Child Abuse and Neglect 14*, 151–163.

Thomas, P. (2005) 'Dissociation and Internal Models of Protection: Psychotherapy with Child Abuse Survivors'. *Psychotherapy, Theory, Resources, Practice, Training 42*, 20–26.

Trinder, L., Beek, M. and Connolly, J. (2002) *Making Contact: How Parents and Children Negotiate and Experience Contact after Divorce*. York: Joseph Rowntree Foundation.

Trotter, C. (2004) *Helping Abused Children and Their Families*. London: Sage.

Walby, S. and Allen, J. (2004) *Domestic Violence, Sexual Assault and Stalking: Findings from the British Crime Survey*. Home Office Research Study 276. London: Home Office.

Walby, S. and Myhill, A. (2002) 'Assessing and Managing Risk'. In J. Taylor-Browne (ed.) *What Works in Reducing Domestic Violence?* London: Whiting and Birch.

Websdale, D. (1999) *Understanding Domestic Homicide*. London: Home Office.

Websdale, N. (2000) *Lethality Assessment Tools: A Critical Analysis*. VAWnet. National Resource Centre on Domestic Violence.

Wetsdale, N., Sheeran, M. and Johnson, B. (1999) *Reviewing Domestic Fatalities: Summarising National Developments.* Online at www.vaw.umn.edu/FinalDocuments/facility.htm. Accessed June 2006.

Weinehall, K. (1997) 'To Grow Up in the Vicinity of Violence: Young People's Stories about Domestic Violence'. *Akademiska avhandlingar vid Pedagogiska institutionen,* Umea universitet, *45,* 328–342.

Williamson, E. (2000) *Domestic Violence and Health.* Bristol: Policy Press.

Wilson, M. and Daly, M. (1998) 'Lethal and Non-Lethal Violence against Wives'. In R. Dobash and R. Dobash (eds) *Re-Thinking Violence against Women.* Thousand Oaks, CA: Sage.

Wolfe, D.A., Jaffe, P., Wilson, S. and Zak, L. (1985) 'Children of Battered Women: The Relation of Child Behaviour to Family Violence and Maternal Stress'. *Journal of Consulting and Clinical Psychology 53,* 5, 657–665.

Young, J. (1999) *The Exclusive Society.* London: Sage.

# Subject Index

Pages in *italics* refer to figures and tables.

# Author Index